SHORT WALKS FROM
—— PUBS IN ——
The Surrey Hills

Derek Palmer

COUNTRYSIDE BOOKS
NEWBURY, BERKSHIRE

First published 1996
© Derek Palmer 1996

COUNTRYSIDE BOOKS
3 Catherine Road
Newbury, Berkshire

ISBN 1 85306 434 3

Designed by Mon Mohan
Cover illustration by Colin Doggett
Photographs and maps by the author

Produced through MRM Associates Ltd., Reading
Printed by Woolnough Bookbinding, Irthlingborough

Contents

Introduction   6

Walk 1   Tilford: The Donkey (2½ or 3½ miles)   8

2   Puttenham: The Good Intent (3½ miles)   12

3   Shackleford: The Cyder House Inn (2½ miles)   17

4   Witley: The White Hart Hotel (4 miles)   21

5   Shalford: The Seahorse Inn (2½ or 3 miles)   26

6   Shamley Green: The Bricklayers Arms (2½ miles)   31

7   West Clandon: The Bull's Head (3 miles)   35

8   Albury: The Drummond Arms (3 miles)   41

9   Shere: The Prince of Wales (3 miles)   45

10   West Horsley: The King William IV (3 or 5 miles)   49

11   Abinger Common: The Abinger Hatch (2 or 2¾ miles)   54

12   Westcott: The Crown Inn (2½ miles)   59

13   Mickleham: The Running Horses (3½ miles)   63

14   Blackbrook: The Plough at Blackbrook (3 miles)   67

15   Brockham: The Royal Oak (2½ or 3 miles)   72

16   Reigate Heath: The Skimmington Castle (3 miles)   77

17 Lower Kingswood: The Mint Arms (2½ miles)   81

18 Chipstead: The Ramblers Rest (2 miles)   85

19 Old Coulsdon: The Fox (3 miles)   89

20 Bletchingley: The Prince Albert (2½ miles)   93

Publisher's Note

We hope that you obtain considerable enjoyment from this book; great care has been taken in its preparation. However, changes of landlord and actual closures are sadly not uncommon. Likewise, although at the time of publication all routes followed public rights of way or permitted paths, diversion orders can be made and permissions withdrawn.

We cannot of course be held responsible for such diversion orders and any inaccuracies in the text which result from these or any other changes to the routes nor any damage which might result from walkers trespassing on private property. We are anxious though that all details covering the walks and the pubs are kept up to date and would therefore welcome information from readers which would be relevant to future editions.

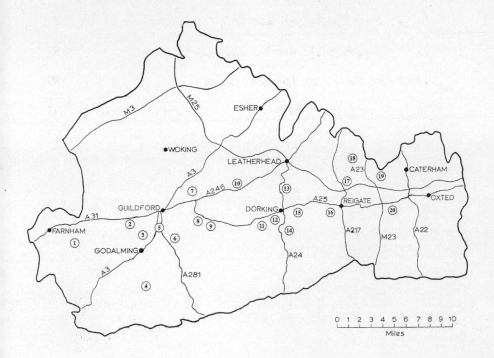

Area map showing the location of the walks.

Introduction

My first experience of organising walks was as a teenager when I lived in London. Once a month I met my pals at either Victoria or Waterloo Station and, with our day return tickets and Spam sandwiches, we travelled to various destinations in Surrey and sallied forth into the countryside. So began my love affair – with its green open spaces and its myriad of paths and bridleways.

Thirty years later, in 1983, I started leading walks in the county once again when a new walking group, the Surrey County Walkers, was formed. The club is still going strong and many friendships have formed there, too. It was with great nostalgia that I began revisiting some of the haunts of my youth. Organising the group led to my subsequently being invited to produce books on walking in the county. The first was *Surrey Rambles*, published in 1987, and, with revisions, it is still in print today. That book was followed by others based on routes from some of the county's favourite country pubs – and here is my third in that series. Researching and writing the books has proved a most pleasurable, and many say enviable, paying hobby!

The temptation to use a good pub again, albeit with a different route, was there but I knew there were others equally suitable. So the quest was on: to select 20 more good pubs with inviting walks close by – and not spread across the county this time but confined to the attractive and popular area of the Surrey Hills! Knowledge built up over many years of walking Surrey's 2,000-plus miles of rights of way has enabled me to find pleasant routes, interesting places to visit and – equally important – first-rate pubs in which to eat and drink! I hope you will be pleased with the result.

The mileage given for each walk should be correct within a ¼ mile or thereabouts. All of the routes are fairly short, mainly around 3 miles, suitable for a family group including young children and for those wanting to walk for an hour or so – two hours at the most. Allow extra time for dallying at viewpoints, taking photographs, having refreshments and stopping at places of interest.

To complement the book the purchase of two Ordnance Survey maps covering all of the areas used would be a worthwhile investment. Landrangers 186 (Aldershot and Guildford) and 187 (Dorking and Reigate) will greatly assist in finding the pubs and the starting points of the walks, for which a map reference is given. They will also enable you to follow the routes. If you enjoy reading maps and want to make your walk even more pleasurable, you may wish to invest in the appropriate OS Pathfinder map(s), details of which are given for each route. At double the scale of the Landrangers, these maps show much more detail. However, maps are not essential since the detailed instructions for each walk, coupled with the use of the sketch map, will ensure you have no difficulty in finding your way.

Directions for locating the pubs are based on the assumption that you are travelling by road and using your own transport. Nevertheless, some of the routes are close to railway stations and Surrey County Council publish timetables for dozens of bus routes that connect the major towns with many of the villages visited on the routes.

As long as you intend to use the pub, all the landlords are willing for their car parks to be used whilst you are away on the walks, but please seek permission before you set off, particularly if you are a large group.

You may not have proper walking shoes or boots and in summer a pair of trainers will probably provide perfectly adequate footwear. However, in winter, and at any time after prolonged rain, paths and particularly bridleways are going to be muddy. Proper walking boots are undoubtedly best but you could possibly get away with wellingtons.

Many pubs would not survive as businesses if locals were their only customers. They rely on passing trade and welcome country walkers. Most walkers are polite, patient and appreciative. Spoiling our image are that small minority who walk across the pub's carpet in muddy boots, expect meals to be produced at the drop of a hat and, worse still, blatantly eat their own food on the premises!

All of the pubs have been chosen not only because they are close to pleasant walking country but also because they offer good value for money in a welcoming and relaxing atmosphere.

As before, thanks are due to my wife, Brenda, who not only assisted me in obtaining the pub information and checking the routes and text but also drew the maps. To her I dedicate this book.

Derek Palmer
Spring 1996

1 Tilford
The Donkey

The Donkey (Morland) is on the former Guildford to Farnham road and, until 1947, was known as the Halfway House, having become an inn in 1730. The building was formed from two cottages constructed of local ironstone. It looks as if it was built in a hollow but it is, in fact, on the side of a hill, Charles Hill to be precise. The donkey connection comes from earlier times when these sturdy beasts helped haul carriages up the hill and were stabled here.

The pub has been run by the same family since 1885. Its interior is interesting, the oak doors and beams having been saved from the demolition of the 14th-century New Inn at Worplesdon. There are two small bars, with plenty of comfortable seating, plus a conservatory with tables for diners. Both bars house much military memorabilia and weaponry, including a rare pair of Japanese duelling daggers as well as a sabre used in the Charge of the Light Brigade. Antique copper and brass, always well-polished, and a collection of old lamps complete the display. Outside is a large garden with flower beds and an aviary, and the inn is famed for its beautiful show of summer flowers.

The standard bar menu offers salads, sandwiches and ploughman's lunches and there are four or five frequently changing, home-made specials, including a vegetarian meal. Fisherman's pie, containing cod, mushrooms and hard-boiled egg, with a potato, cheese and mustard topping, is available every day and is extremely popular. The sweets are home-made locally and there is a choice of four ice-creams. The regular real ales are Morland Old Speckled Hen and Independent IPA and the guest ale is Charles Wells Bombardier. The draught cider is Scrumpy Jack and there is draught Guinness, too. Children are allowed in the conservatory at lunchtimes and in the garden, of course, where there is a play area, but not in the bars if under 14. Well-behaved dogs are welcome.

The pub is open on Monday to Saturday from 11 am to 2.30 pm and 6 pm to 11 pm, and on Sunday from 12 noon to 3 pm and 7 pm to 10.30 pm. Food is served from 12 noon to 2 pm and 7 pm to 9.30 pm (no food on Sunday evenings).

Telephone: 01252 702124.

How to get there: The pub will be found at Charleshill, a mile west of Elstead. It lies on the B3001, which runs between Farnham and the A3 at Milford.

Parking: With permission, you are welcome to use the pub's car park whilst on your walk. It is not large and soon fills up, so take a tip and get there early.

Length of the walk: About 3½ miles in total, but it can be reduced by a mile if need be. However, this would mean missing the attractive Tilford Green. OS maps: Landranger 186 Aldershot and Guildford or Pathfinder 1225 Farnham and Godalming (inn GR 893444).

Halfway round the walk you arrive at Tilford Green, always popular with walkers, cricketers and sightseers, with its ancient bridge over the Wey and famous oak. The well-defined paths to and from the green, besides offering frequent good views, are a delight in themselves.

The Walk

1   From the pub entrance turn left onto a bridleway, shortly reaching a junction of paths and continuing round to the left. Your wide, sandy, tree-lined track is cut from a deep slope and later, as it rises, you reach a more open area, dotted with pine trees. Here you are afforded excellent southerly views across to Hindhead Common, with Blackdown, the highest point in Sussex, beyond.

2   You reach a residential road with the entrance to a grand house, Whitmead, on your left. Take the lower, downhill, fork. Eventually the road begins to climb and you come to a turning on the right.

For the shorter walk, turn right here and continue with the instructions in the second sentence of 4. This will, however, mean missing Tilford Green.

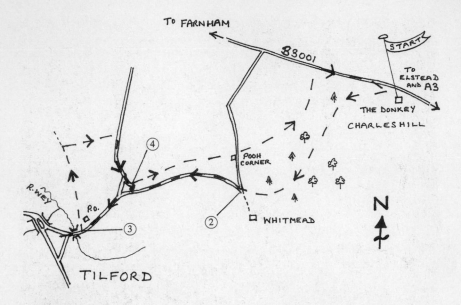

For the main walk, you continue beyond the turning and reach a main road, which you cross, turning left along the footpath. Shortly, if you look across to the field opposite, you may see a large assortment of farm animals, including sheep, goats and pigs. Pass by a garage and the Tilford village post office/village store, where confectionery, drinks and ice-creams are available. Now go over the river Wey via an ancient bridge and onto Tilford Green.

The bridges here (there is another at the far end of the green, taking the road over the other branch of the river Wey) are thought to have been built by monks from nearby Waverley Abbey. This was the first Cistercian monastery in the country, now standing in ruins a mile away, to the north. The confluence of the rivers Wey and Till is behind the Barley Mow which, having been around for over 200 years, is the oldest of Tilford's three pubs. The triangular green has been well known for its cricket pitch for 100 years or more. Rather than bow to their opponents' superior skill, losing teams tend to blame the unevenness of the pitch and their batsmen's inability to see the bowlers commence their run. The famous Tilford Oak, merely an acorn in the middle 1600s, is still standing – but only just!

3 After taking a short rest, resume the walk by retracing your steps over the bridge. Immediately before the post office, turn left onto a public bridleway. The path is quite tunnel-like in places, giving shelter from the sun and, better still, from the rain. Later your track becomes tarred and narrower, then, in a total of a little over ¼ mile, reaches a driveway. Turn sharp right on the driveway, which is also a public bridleway, enjoying

10

Tilford cottage

views on the left over to the Hog's Back. In about ¼ mile you will reach a road on which you turn right. Pass a small housing estate on your right and Hazelwood Nursery on the left. The road curves left and then right where you reach a turning on the left.

4   Turn left past Marley Cottage and, where this road bears right (and would lead you back onto your outward route), you reach a private road. Join the road which is the driveway to Lane House, Tile House and Archers Hill and is also a public footpath. When you reach the entrance to Archers Hill, drop down from the driveway to continue on the narrow footpath on the right. Later your path widens and bears left past a house called Pooh Corner, where you cross a road, continuing on a public footpath. The path continues downhill with a fence on the right. Go through a metal kissing-gate and continue on an enclosed path, over a drive to a junction of driveways. Keep ahead on a path running parallel with a drive on the left and a stone wall on the right. Your path joins another drive and you reach a road. Turn right along the road, taking care and keeping well into the right. Just before reaching 'road narrows' and 'right bend' signs, bear right onto a bridleway going downhill. Go over a driveway towards a wall and turn left onto the track that formed the beginning of your walk. In no time at all you'll be back at the pub.

2 Puttenham
The Good Intent

The Good Intent (Grand Met) is a listed building dating from the 16th century and has been a pub for over 200 years. Judging from the archway, it may have been an overnight stop for stagecoaches on the road which ran between Guildford and Farnham long before the Hog's Back (A31) was opened. It makes no pretensions of being anything other than a friendly village pub, popular with locals and visitors alike and particularly with walkers doing the North Downs Way.

There is a large, semi-circular bar divided into three sections. One area contains a pool table and other pub games, another a pleasant, fairly basic bar and the third a cosy lounge with a splendid inglenook fireplace. Each year on 1st November the welcoming log fire is lit and it is not allowed to go out until 30th March of the following year. Those who are dining tend to use the lounge with its exposed beams and snug corners.

About half of the food is home-prepared and besides a comprehensive bar menu, including a whole assortment of snacks such as ploughman's lunches and sandwiches, there are plenty of specials on the board – for example, braised beef, a seafood special or gammon steak. Traditional sweets are much in evidence and you might find favourites such as spotted dick and chocolate sponge with custard or ice-cream. On Wednesday evenings from 6 pm until 9 pm (earlier if they run out!) the place is turned into a fish 'n' chip shop – eat in or take away! The regular real ales in this country inn are Courage Best, Wadworth 6X and Old Speckled Hen and the guest might be Hogs Back TEA or APB, Hampshire King Alfred's or Ringwood Best. The landlord takes his ales very seriously and displays forthcoming brews on a blackboard on the bar. Draught Guinness is available and cider drinkers should be warned – besides Blackthorn there's Inch's, an incredible concoction at 8% alcoholic volume! Children are only allowed in the garden but dogs on leads are permitted in the bars.

The pub is open on Monday to Friday from 11 am to 2.30 pm and 6 pm to 11 pm, on Saturday from 11 am to 11 pm, and on Sunday from 12 noon to 3 pm and 7 pm to 10.30 pm. Food is served at lunchtime every day from 12 noon to 2 pm. In the evening on Tuesday and on Thursday to Saturday it is available from 7 pm to 10 pm, and on Wednesday from 6 pm to 9 pm. Note: There is no food on Sunday and Monday evenings.

Telephone: 01483 810387.

How to get there: Take the B3000 to Puttenham, signposted from the A31 Hog's Back Guildford to Farnham road and the A3 Portsmouth road. After entering the village you will soon find the pub on the right.

Parking: The pub has a small car park which is reached through an archway. With permission, you are welcome to use it whilst on your walk. Space can also usually be found along the road, where there are no restrictions.

Length of the walk: About 3½ miles. OS maps: Landranger 186 Aldershot and Guildford or Pathfinder 1225 Farnham and Godalming (inn GR 932477).

Starting from a typical, appealing Surrey village you are led through woods and across farmland to Wanborough, one of the county's unique hamlets – a tiny place, with delightful buildings and absorbing history. Admittedly, you need to cross an extremely busy road twice, but within minutes of leaving it you could be a million miles away!

The Walk

1   From the pub turn right along the street for a few yards and then right again on School Lane. After you pass the school the tar runs out and you continue on an uphill bridleway. Climb steadily on this track, which offers plenty of shade from the sun (or shelter from the rain!). Close to the top of the slope you will reach a fork. Do not use the permissive horse-ride on the left but keep right and soon come out to the A31 dual carriageway.

2   Before crossing (with great care) the west-bound carriageway, look back at what, on a fine day, will be a magnificent view. Having crossed to

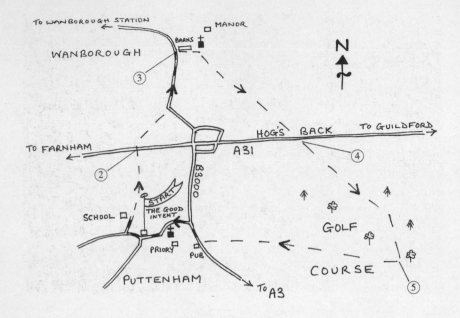

the central reservation, turn left for a few yards and go through an opening in the hedge. Again with great care, cross the east-bound carriageway and turn right along the grass for about 50 yards. Here you turn left over a stile (dilapidated when we crossed it) by a public footpath sign. Fork diagonally right across a field, usually in crop with corn in high summer, and reach a road. Turn left along a raised footpath into Wanborough.

Wanborough is a lovely hamlet nestled against the hillside. The name is said to come from Werna's or Wodin's Bergh (hill) and this was once a place of pagan worship. The local fields are full of flint and Neolithic tools have been found in the area.

3   In a few yards, just before the road turns sharply left, cross onto a wide farm track past some ancient tithe barns. The larger barn is exceptional for Surrey, measuring 95 ft by 30 ft. The Cistercian monks of Waverley Abbey built it, using it for the storage of wool from their flocks. Notice the Victorian postbox in the wall.

Just beyond the barns you reach the tiny church of St Bartholomew. The interior measurements of the church, once a 13th-century flint chapel built on the site of a Domesday building, are just 44½ by 18 ft. It fell into disrepair in the 17th century, was then used for farm storage purposes, and in 1861-2 was restored by a Mr Duckworth, the Rector of Puttenham.

In the 19th century the tenant at Wanborough Manor, by the church, was Sir Algernon West, Prime Minister Gladstone's Parliamentary Private Secretary, and cabinet meetings were held here. Early in the 20th century

14

Tithe barns, Wanborough

another prime minister, Asquith, was a sub-tenant and two of his daughters are buried in the churchyard. During World War II the house was used for planning secret operations in Europe (SOE) and the training of agents destined for placement in Nazi-occupied Europe.

To continue the walk, opposite the church fork right onto a public bridleway and continue along for about ½ mile. Before reaching the main road again you should find some uninterrupted views across to Guildford and, on a clear day, the tall buildings of Woking can be seen. Cross the east-bound carriageway, turn left and then go right, through an opening under the trees. Cross the west-bound carriageway to a fingerpost opposite and go over a stile.

4   Walk down the left side of a field, go over a stile into another field and then over another stile. Continue over a track and another stile, then go diagonally right across a field to the next stile, in front of a dilapidated barn, soon crossing yet another stile. You enter a golf course and head for a potentially obscured and overgrown path on the left. You will find yourself crossing two or three golfing fairways, so take care and continue your route by following through a series of white posts. Eventually you go alongside a garden fence and reach a track.

5   Turn right along the track, which forms part of the North Downs Way and runs along the edge of the older part of Puttenham Golf Course. You remain on this track for about ¾ mile and eventually pass the clubhouse.

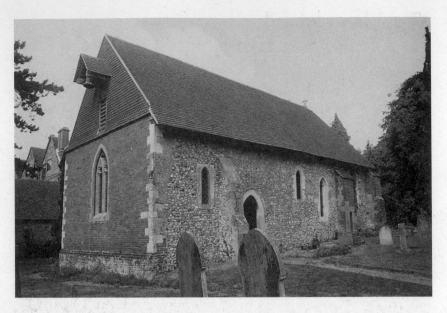

The tiny church of St Bartholomew, Wanborough.

Beyond a metal barn you reach a road, with the Jolly Farmer opposite. Turn right along the footpath and then cross the road to the raised footway opposite. Bear left back into Puttenham village and the pub.

On your way you will find many attractive tile-hung and timber-framed houses, some built in the 14th and 15th centuries. The church of St John the Baptist dates from about 1160, but was much restored in 1861. The well in the churchyard was discovered in 1972 when a cypress tree subsided into it – it had been filled in more than 200 years earlier.

You should also catch a glimpse of Puttenham Priory, dating from 1762, a fine Palladian mansion and the site of a much earlier house, part of the manor of Puttenham. This came into the Prior of Newark's possession in 1248, hence the house's name. There was never a monastic foundation here and the house was at one time in the ownership of Sir Edward Hulton, the founder of *Picture Post* magazine. In 1950 it became an old people's home and was sold again 26 years later. In 1995 it was completely refurbished and turned into an extremely smart commercial and residential complex.

3 Shackleford
The Cyder House Inn

The Cyder House Inn (freehouse) was built in the late 19th century by the Governor of the Bank of England at that time. The original Cyder House became enclosed within his property and, under the terms of the planning agreement, he was required to build a new public house for the villagers. The original Cyder House remains within the grounds of the school opposite.

Considerable alterations have taken place in recent years and, unlike the usual pub furniture, everything here is made of pine, creating a light and airy feel to the place. The name 'Cyder House Inn' has become a misnomer since no apples are crushed and fermented here. Instead, various real ales (only sold here) are produced in the micro brewery and, for those who are interested, tours can be booked in advance.

The house prides itself on its choice of bitters. There are always at least six real ales, including one of the home brews, on offer. As may be expected, draught cider – Sweet and Dry Blackthorn as well as the deadly Inch's Scrumpy – are also served. Draught Guinness and house wines sold by the glass are amongst the extensive range of other drinks. The food, virtually all home-prepared, is of a high standard, but without high prices to match. The young managers make frequent early visits to Smithfield and Billingsgate markets in central London to buy their meat and fish, and the choice of mouth-watering dishes is wide. Besides the usual pub favourites, there are many less common dishes from which to make your selection, and any special dietary needs can be catered for, with advance notice. Children have their own fixed-price menu and are welcome inside the pub.

Outside you will find a nice patio and garden area with tables. There's a dog in residence, so just check with the staff before bringing in your own.

The pub is open on Monday to Friday from 11 am to 3 pm and 5.30 pm to 11 pm, on Saturday from 11 am to 11 pm, and on Sunday from 12 noon to 10.30 pm. Food is served on Monday to Friday from 12 noon to 2.30 pm and 7 pm to 9 pm. On Saturday and Sunday blackboard meals are available between 12 noon and 2.30 pm, basket meals between 2.30 pm and 4.30 pm, and from 7 pm to 9.30 pm the evening menu applies.

Telephone: 01483 810360.

How to get there: Leave the A3 London to Portsmouth road about 4 miles south of Guildford, at the exit signposted to Shackleford. Follow the signs for Shackleford and in under a mile reach the village centre and a road junction by the post office/village store. Turn left here on Peper Harow Lane and find the pub in just a few yards on the left.

Parking: There is a large car park which you are welcome to use whilst on your walk, but please let the staff know.

Length of the walk: About 2½ miles. OS maps: Landranger 186 Aldershot and Guildford or Pathfinder 1225 Farnham and Godalming (inn GR 935452).

The route runs through a conservation area of outstanding natural beauty. It takes you through an estate village, full of atmosphere, which would happily lend itself as a location for a period film set. It is not difficult to imagine the squire and his estate workers decked out in their Sunday best on the way to the little church.

The Walk
1   From the pub turn right down the road, soon reaching a junction by the village post office/store, where you turn right along Grenville Road. In a couple of hundred yards fork left onto Rokers Lane. You pass some houses and continue along a wide track for about ⅓ mile, where you reach a waymarked post.
2   Fork right onto the bridleway and after about ¼ mile your track leads you to a road junction. Cross over to the far road (School Lane), signposted to Norney, and turn right. In another ¼ mile you reach a T-junction at Norney Farm. Turn right along the pavement past the school

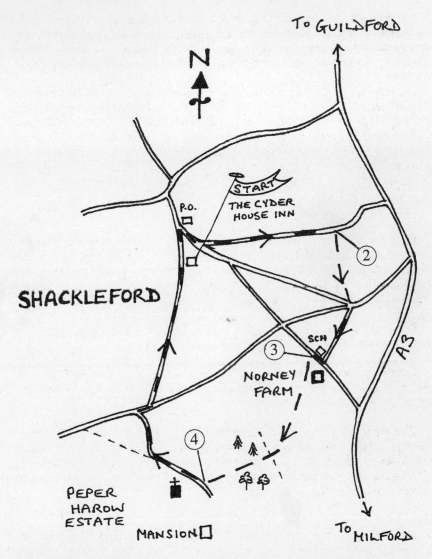

and, in less than 100 yards, cross the road to a footpath fingerpost on the left.

3 Turn left on the footpath and, after going along the end of some gardens, reach a waymarked stile which you cross. Bear diagonally right across a field, passing an interesting tree on your left. Cross a stile leading into another field and maintain direction across it to a wooden barrier/horse jump with horizontal pales and a fingerpost in a line of trees.

Shackleford village stores and post office

Pass over a track and go through a snatch of woodland to cross a stile. Go straight ahead over a field, crossing another stile leading into the next field. Head for a stile to the left of a large metal barn and pass some Cedars of Lebanon, which were planted as seedlings from pots, to arrive at a roadway running through the Peper Harow estate.

There's been a settlement here for many centuries but the estate village as you see it today was formed in 1735. The mansion was for many years a Surrey County Council special school. Built in 1775 on the site of the original mansion, this building was near-gutted by a serious fire in the 1980s.

4   Turn right past a muddy duck pond, continuing along the road past the church on the left. Trees in the attractive churchyard date from between 800 and 1,300 years ago and among those buried here is Sir Henry Dalrymple White who led the Charge of the Heavy Brigade at Balaclava. Soon look for the 18th-century estate cottages and granary through the gateway on the right. The granary was raised on stilts to prevent the depredations of rodents. You go through a gateway, past a public footpath fingerpost on the left, and follow the estate roadway as it curves left, bringing you out to a road. Turn right for a few yards and then left on the road signposted to Shackleford and Puttenham. Continue down the road for about ½ mile and you are back at the pub.

4 Witley
The White Hart Hotel

The White Hart Hotel (freehouse) is a friendly pub and an ancient one, though not, these days, a hotel. The inn, built for King Richard II in 1380, was granted a licence in 1700 and most definitely houses a ghost – in fact two, one male and one female! Framed pencil portraits of the couple hang in the saloon bar. The artist said she saw the woman on the pub stairs and the man in one of the bedrooms. When the pub's owners took over in 1994 a well-known medium and a dowser confirmed the ghosts' presence. Legend also has it that Nelson and Lady Hamilton used the pub for some of their secret assignations and it is a fact that George Eliot, who lived nearby, was a regular customer. The novelist is said to have written some of her best known works here, including *The Mill on the Floss* and her last work, *Daniel Deronda*.

The pub comprises a saloon bar, low-beamed with an uneven floor and attractive fireplace, a separate dining room and a small public bar, complete with games. The landlord is also a musician, playing clarinet and tenor saxophone, and on an evening visit you may catch him with his traditional jazz band. Outside there is a large beer garden, complete with children's attractions including swings and a roundabout. Children are welcome in the dining room and dogs are permitted in the bars, but not the other way round.

The wide range of food is excellent here – all home-cooked and served in generous portions. The blackboard displays a number of dishes, which will probably include pies such as steak and kidney in ale or chicken and leek, and the regular menu contains the usual pub favourites, basket meals, ploughman's lunches, sandwiches, and jacket potatoes. Vegetarians, too, have a good selection, for example, courgette and mushroom stroganoff or egg and spinach lasagne verdi. Tea, as well as coffee, is available and children have their own menu. The desserts are home-made and there is a variety of ice-creams to choose from. A special lunch is on offer for OAPs on a Wednesday. The regular real ale is Brakspear Bitter and the frequently changing guest ales might include Abbot Ale and Hogs Back TEA. The draught cider is Dry Blackthorn, Guinness also comes through a pump and one red and two white wines are available by the glass.

The pub is open on Monday to Saturday from 11 am to 2.30 pm and 5.30 pm to 11 pm, and on Sunday from 12 noon to 3 pm and 7 pm to 10.30 pm, all day on Saturday and Sunday in summer. Food is served on Monday to Friday from 11.30 am to 2.30 pm and 6 pm to 10 pm, on Saturday from 11.30 am to 3 pm and 6 pm to 10 pm, and on Sunday from 12 noon to 3 pm and 7 pm to 9.30 pm.

Telephone: 01428 683695.

How to get there: Witley lies on the A283 Milford to Petworth road, 2 miles south of the A3 at Milford. If travelling south, you will find the pub on the left-hand side, soon after entering Witley. Alternatively, the walk could be commenced from Witley Station, situated between Points 3 and 4, visiting the pub at the halfway stage.

Parking: There is an adequate car park which, with permission, you are welcome to use whilst on the walk.

Length of the walk: About 4 miles. OS maps: Landranger 186 Aldershot and Guildford or Pathfinder 1245 Haslemere and Hindhead (inn GR 948397).

This route is largely through woodland but with plenty of gaps in the trees offering fine views. Apart from having a busy main road running through it, the 20th century has hardly touched the village of Witley, a conservation area, which has retained many of its old buildings.

The Walk

1   From the pub cross over the road to the pavement opposite and turn left. Shortly you will find Chichester Hall over on your left and here you need to re-cross the road to enter a large recreation ground. There's an impressive copper beech tree on your right as you walk towards the

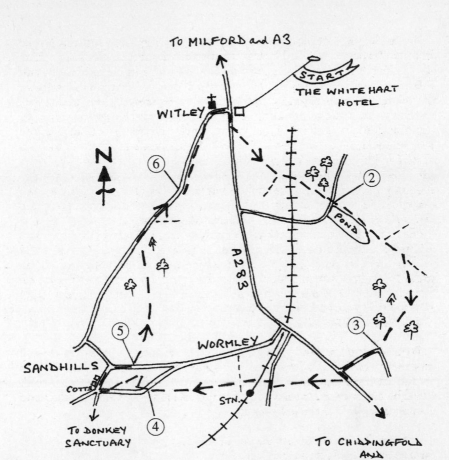

TO MILFORD and A3

WITLEY

START
THE WHITE HART
HOTEL

N

⑥

②

POND

A283

⑤

WORMLEY

③

SANDHILLS

COTTS

STN.

TO DONKEY
SANCTUARY

④

TO CHIDDINGFOLD
AND
PETWORTH

children's play area. Pass a fence on your left, leaving the recreation ground in the bottom corner. Ignore a turning on the right and pass a garage on your left, maintaining direction on a narrow log path and shortly going over a footbridge. The woodland path takes you under the railway and bears right. In about ¼ mile you reach a road.

2   Cross the road slightly right to a driveway which takes you along the side of the very pretty Sweetwater Pond. (If you would like to have a better view of the pond, continue down the road for a few yards and then retrace your steps.) In about ⅓ mile ignore a bridleway forking left and other left turns. Keep close to the fence of Buss's Cottage as this very sandy path curves round to the right. At the next bridleway sign continue left, ignoring a footpath opening on the right. You reach a junction of several tracks by the half-timbered More Cottage and turn right on the

Witley church.

lower, permissive, bridlepath. Later ignore another permissive horse ride on your left and come down to a road.

3 Turn right along the road and in ¼ mile, after passing riding stables on your left, reach the main road. Cross over, turn left, and in a few yards turn right by a fingerpost, through a metal barrier, onto an enclosed path which forms part of the Greensand Way. You go along a series of tree-formed 'tunnels' and through another barrier out to a road at Wormley. There is a village store and the car park for Witley railway station opposite but you turn right along the pavement for a few yards and then cross the road to a fingerpost and public footpath. Shortly you cross the railway via a footbridge and continue on a narrow footpath with a fence on the left. Walk over a crossing track and along a path until in about another ½ mile, after passing a large wooden barn and going through some wooden posts, you reach a road.

4 Cross over onto a track and turn right at a Greensand Way marker, passing a garden with an ornate fence, then climb up a slope. At the top turn left, leaving the Greensand Way for a while, and admire views across to Blackdown, the highest point in Sussex. Shortly, join a wide track coming in from the left which leads you back down to the road near a telephone box at Sandhills. Continue forward along the road for a few yards and on the opposite side you'll see a turning on the left leading to the Lockwood Donkey Sanctuary. (If you have children in tow you may like

Step Cottage, Witley – with the ancient church to the rear.

to take some time out of your walk to stop here. It is open from 9 am to 5.30 pm every day. For further information telephone 01428 682409.) To continue the walk turn right on Sebastapol Road past the pretty Rose Cottage and Step Cottage – both buildings of historic interest. You reach a road junction with an island and turn right, still enjoying good views across to Blackdown. In about 200 yards you will find a public bridleway on the left.

5   Turn left past Woodbury Cottage, back once again on the Greensand Way. You pass a gateway and a stile on the right and, in about ½ mile, reach a road on which you turn right. Pass a half-timbered house on your left, Winkford Grange, and go past a footpath turning by Hangerfield Cottage on your right.

6   Immediately after passing a large house, Hangerfield, turn right, joining a public footpath running parallel with the road. Part of the time you are above the road, where you are close to the exposed, gnarled roots of beech trees perched precariously on top of the bank. Along the way you'll find a handy seat if you want to sit and take in the views for a short while. Your path joins a driveway and leads you down to the road, on which you turn right. Shortly you pass Witley's Domesday church and another Step Cottage to find yourself back at the pub.

5 Shalford
The Seahorse Inn

The Seahorse Inn (Gale's) dates from the 17th century and was a farmhouse with an adjacent inn. There was still a farm here as relatively recently as the 1920s, then the building was renovated and it has remained essentially the same ever since. It is thought that the name was probably taken from one of the farm cottages and derived from the fact that the old tavern once served as a coaching inn. It is suggested that this is where the London-bound coaches changed horses – sea horses from the coast being replaced by land horses for the remaining journey to London. This could be a bit of a fairy tale as the pub is a mile or so from the old London to Portsmouth road. However, the story suits the brewery, which happens to be based in Horndean, close to Portsmouth.

You enter the pub through a mini museum – on one side ancient brewing equipment and on the other the stables as they may have looked a century or so ago. The pub today is a pleasant inn with wood-panelled walls and plenty of old beams. The first bar, where the food servery is found, functions as a family room and dining area for non-smokers. This leads into a much larger bar/dining room, off which there is another bar, complete with fruit machine, dartboard and pool table.

There's a good range of pub grub, including several sandwich choices, jacket potatoes with a variety of fillings and some very special ploughman's lunches called 'platters'. Main meals are shown on blackboards and may include home-cooked beef and ale pie and ham. Those who like to share should try the huge 'platter for two'. If two adults are eating and are accompanied by a child, the little one's meal comes free. Regular visitors can ask for a diner's card. Every time you have a meal the card is marked and after four meals the next is on the house. The resident real ales all come up from Horndean and are HSB, Best and Butser Brew Bitter. There's a periodically changing guest ale, too. The draught Irish stout is Beamish and the ciders are Dry Blackthorn and Cidermaster. Wines, including Gale's country wines – and there is a choice of 21 – are served by the glass. Children are, of course, welcome in the family room. Dogs must be confined to the bar, away from the dining areas. Outside there is a large garden with plenty of seats and tables as well as play equipment.

The pub is open on Monday to Friday from 11.30 am to 3 pm and 5.30 pm to 11 pm, on Saturday from 11 am to 11 pm, and on Sunday from 12 noon to 10.30 pm. Food is served on Monday to Saturday from 12 noon to 2 pm and 6.30 pm to 9.30 pm, and at lunchtime on Sunday.

Telephone: 01483 61917.

How to get there: Shalford is a mile or so south of Guilford on the A281 Horsham road. The pub is near the church, on the same side of the road. Alternatively, the walk could be commenced from Shalford Station at Point 2.

Parking: The pub has two large car parks which you are welcome to use whilst on the walk, but please seek permission.

Length of the walk: About 3 miles (or 2½ miles if you take the shorter route). OS maps: Landranger 186 Aldershot and Guildford or Pathfinders 1226 Dorking and (small part only) 1225 Farnham and Godalming (inn GR 000476).

Although close to the busy town of Guildford, you soon escape onto some pleasant farmland paths, offering good views of the North Downs and beyond. At the end of the walk you can look around the 18th-century Shalford Mill, now in the care of the National Trust.

The Walk

1 From the pub turn left and immediately left again onto a bridleway. Where the bridleway forks go right for a few yards and then turn left onto a narrow path with a fence running alongside. You will have occasional glimpses of meadows (often flooded in winter) along the banks of the river Wey. The path bears right but you keep ahead, still following the fence,

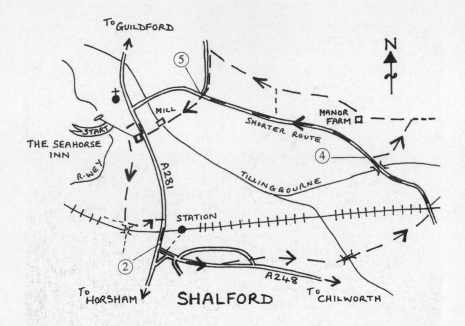

until you reach a kissing-gate. Join the parallel bridleway and maintain direction. As you approach a railway bridge with a sign warning that laden weight is not to exceed nine tons (have you already eaten?) turn left onto a narrow path running along the side of the railway. You emerge onto a green which you cross to the road ahead. Here you turn right over the railway bridge and then cross the road via a pelican crossing.

2 Turn right and go past the turning leading down to Shalford Station, bearing left onto Kings Road and continuing for about ¼ mile. When you reach a green, keep ahead on the tarred path, crossing a roadway and passing cottages over on your left. Eventually the tarred path runs out and you continue on a gravelled driveway. Soon bear left onto a tarred driveway, shortly going over a bridge. You reach a two-way fingerpost and leave the main path, passing a stile on your right and going through a barrier, then continuing along the side of a large sports field. Eventually you arrive at a level-crossing.

3 Cross the track and continue on the lane ahead. You pass a sawmill, the lane curves left and goes past some houses. A brick bridge takes you over the Tillingbourne and in a few more yards you discover a stile leading to a footpath turning off to the right.

For the shorter route, continue ahead on the lane for a little over ½ mile to meet the main walk at Point 5.

Shalford Mill.

4   Having crossed the stile, take the uphill footpath and cross another stile, with its unusually high three steps each side, and head diagonally right across a large field. At the other side go over a stile and turn left onto a hedged farm track. You arrive at Manor Farm, turning right over a stile then immediately left along the side of a field. Ahead you will see the green spire of Shalford church and, after passing a footpath turning across the field on your left, you should have a good view on your right over to Guildford Cathedral on the skyline. If the fields have been freshly ploughed you'll notice that the earth is quite red here – almost putting you in mind of Devon soil. At the end of this very long field you go over a stile and turn left along a path running parallel with a residential road, eventually leading you back to the lane.

5 Go up the steps opposite, over a stile and across a field, shortly with a wire fence on your right. Cross another stile and continue on an enclosed footpath, arriving at Shalford Mill which, with much of its machinery intact, is well worth visiting (open daily from 10 am to 5pm).

In the care and ownership of the National Trust since 1932 this 18th-century watermill is one of the most appealing in the county. Formerly in the possession of one of Surrey's largest landowners, the Godwin-Austen family, the charming timber-framed building has brick walls to first floor height and tile-hung side walls. The sacks of corn were lifted into the mill by the sack hoist in the large overhanging storey. The mill pond was previously located in the field on the south side of the mill. The control sluice to the bypass culvert can be seen by the side of the footpath leading to the field.

Having visited the mill continue on the lane ahead back to the A281 and the pub opposite. Before crossing the road, look at the concrete structure to the left of the pub. It was erected during World War II and was designed to hold a barrier across the road in order to thwart the advance of an anticipated invasion force.

A short way along the road you will see the Victorian church, built on the site of a Domesday church, with its attractive spire and the village stocks outside. The pretty cottages opposite give an impression of how the village would have looked before the age of the motor car. Behind the church the Tillingbourne flows into the river Wey.

6 Shamley Green
The Bricklayers Arms

The Bricklayers Arms (Courage) has always been appreciated by wayfarers and remains welcoming to ramblers to this day. Originally it was called the Top House and was Shamley Green's (Shamble Lea, when Oliver Cromwell granted the village a charter for an annual fair) first pub. The oldest part goes back over 200 years and the ceiling beams and plastered walls confirm the building's antiquity. Unpretentious in every way, it claims to be nothing other than a typical village local, as the regular clientele will testify. However, many walking groups make good use of it too, finding the atmosphere friendly and comfortable.

All the hot food available is written on the blackboard. This usually comprises about six different dishes, including pot meals like macaroni cheese or potato, Stilton and leek bake, chilli with rice and omelette with chips. The usual walkers' favourites such as ploughman's lunches, jacket potatoes and sandwiches are also available, as is a bowl of soup and a roll in winter. There is always something for vegetarians and children's portions are served. The regular real ales are Courage Best and Gale's HSB, alongside a guest beer. Olde English cider comes through a pump and draught Guinness is offered. A few chilled wines are also dispensed for sale by the glass. Children and dogs are allowed in the pub. Outside there is also a beer garden, swings and other play equipment.

The pub is open on Monday to Saturday from 11.30 am to 11 pm, and on Sunday from 12 noon to 10.30 pm. Food is served every day from 12 noon to 2.30 pm and 6.30 pm to 10 pm.
Telephone: 01483 898377.

How to get there: Shamley Green lies on the B2128 between Cranleigh and the A248 at Shalford, south of Guildford. The pub is on the edge of the large village green.

Parking: With permission, you are welcome to use the car park whilst on the walk. If this is full there is plenty of parking space around the green.

Length of the walk: About 2½ miles. OS maps: Landranger 186 Aldershot and Guildford or Pathfinder 1226 Dorking (inn GR 034437).

Here is another ramble which uses a section of the Greensand Way and where, for much of the time, the hills of Surrey form a background to the views. This village has one of the county's largest greens, criss-crossed by

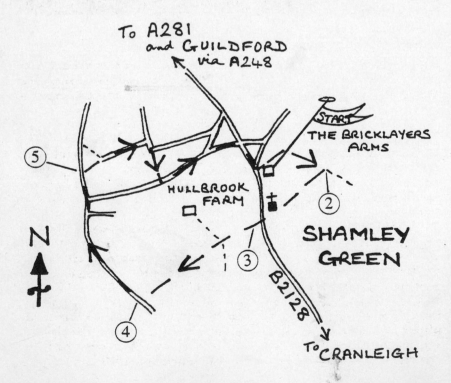

Christ Church, Shamley Green

little lanes, with houses in many styles around its perimeter. Cricket is played here every summer weekend, creating a picturesque scene. The church, somewhat isolated from this tableau, is passed a little way into the walk.

The Walk

1   From the pub turn right along the side of the green. In a few yards you reach a metal fingerpost at the entrance to Summer Meadow and turn right onto a narrow footpath enclosed by fences. Eventually go over a stile and the path, still narrow, continues along the side of a field. Shortly you arrive at a stile and a cattle trough on your right.

2   Cross the stile, joining a section of the Greensand Way. Keeping a fence to your left, continue along the side of the field to another stile which leads you onto a fenced path running between fields. After crossing the next stile you shortly come to the remains of a kissing-gate and continue on a path running alongside the churchyard.

When funerals take place at Christ Church it is customary for a penny to be placed on the gatepost. It is considered that if this ritual does not take place as the coffin is carried into the churchyard an indisputable right of way will be established. Although only dating from Victorian times, the church has many interesting and unusual features both inside and out.

3 From the church cross the road with care and go through a small parking area, passing the vicarage on your left. Join a bridleway, shown as a 'horse ride', and after ¼ mile go through a metal gate and across a farm track. Continue in the same direction between fields ahead and, after enjoying fine views of the surrounding countryside, in a further ¼ mile go through another metal gate to reach a tarred roadway.

4 Turn right along the roadway, thus leaving the Greensand Way, passing some attractive houses on your left. Eventually you pass a drive leading to Hullbrook Farm on the right and immediately another right turn and you still continue ahead. Shortly you pass a turning on the left, just before a row of modern houses, and arrive at a green which has children's play equipment over to the left.

5 In a few yards bear right through wooden posts onto a tarred footpath where there are some older houses on your right. You reach a red telephone box and Victorian letterbox and continue up a residential road to a T-junction. Turn right and, where the road turns left, go straight ahead on a driveway leading to a path enclosed by a fence and hedge. You are led out to a road, where you turn left along the footway. Shortly you arrive back at the green and bear right, passing Arbuthnot Hall and the village post office and stores. Turn right at the main road to return to the pub.

7 West Clandon
The Bull's Head

The Bull's Head (Courage), a former Tudor hall house, dates from 1530, the front elevation being Grade II listed. Experts have confirmed the date from the way in which the supporting oak beams were placed. Apparently, from 1535 onwards they were positioned with the root end at the bottom and prior to that it was uppermost. According to a notice by the pub entrance, a well-known local highwayman, Robert Newland, was at one time known to hang up his pistols here. The sign also suggests that one of the previous licensees did some sleeping on the premises, too!

This pub is popular with locals and visitors alike as a visit on any day of the week will confirm. But it would not be unkind to suggest that you will get 'a load of bull' if you come here. Photographs and drawings, including some amusing cartoons with a bovine connection, abound and there's hardly a wall not covered with them. Even the menus are adorned with delightful sketches executed by a customer – one is of a pipe-smoking bull with an uncanny resemblance to the landlord!

The food is of a high standard but without prices to match. The landlady spends most of her weekends making succulent pies and there are always three or four on offer, served with well-cooked fresh vegetables. Separate menus for lunchtime and evenings are available and all the home-made specials are chalked-up on a blackboard. Walkers and others requiring no more than a tasty snack will find a good range of jacket potatoes, salads, ploughman's lunches and sandwiches (toasted sandwiches in the evening). Most of the sweets are home-made, too, butterscotch tart and banoffi pie coming highly recommended. A children's menu, with all their usual favourites, is also to hand. Courage Best is the obvious regular real ale but there are always two guests. These are likely to be Wadworth 6X and Ruddles County. Strongbow cider and Guinness also come through the pumps and there are wines by the glass. Children and dogs, accompanied by well-behaved adults, are welcome inside the inn. The small beer garden contains some nice attractions for youngsters, including swings and an impressive play house.

The pub is open on Monday to Friday from 11 am to 2.30 pm and 5.30 pm to 11 pm, on Saturday from 11 am to 3 pm and 6 pm to 11 pm, and on Sunday from 12 noon to 3 pm and 7 pm to 10.30 pm. Food is served on Monday to Friday from 12 noon to 2 pm and 6 pm to 9 pm, on Saturday from 12 noon to 2.30 pm and 6 pm to 9 pm, and on Sunday from 12 noon to 2.30 pm only.

Telephone: 01483 222444.

How to get there: If coming from the Guildford (A25) or Leatherhead (A246) direction, leave the dual carriageway where the two roads meet at traffic lights and take the A247, signposted to Woking. The pub is on the left, just after the entrance to Clandon House. If approaching from the north, from Woking or the A3, take the A247 to find the pub on the right, almost a mile beyond Clandon railway station. If travelling by train join the walk at Point 2, about ½ mile from the station.

Parking: There is room for around 25 to 30 cars and, with permission, you are welcome to use the car park whilst on the walk.

Length of the walk: About 3 miles. OS maps: Landranger 186 Aldershot and Guildford and 187 Dorking and Reigate or Pathfinder 1206 Woking and Leatherhead (inn GR 045515).

You commence your walk by going along West Clandon's busy main road, like many other Surrey village thoroughfares named 'The Street'. Along here you'll find a diversity of architecture representative of Tudor times and the centuries following. After leaving the main road your path to East Clandon traverses what once was farmland, more recently transformed into golfing greens and fairways. A quick tour of East Clandon, with its attractive church, and a parallel route brings you back in a westerly direction, taking in West Clandon's church at the end of the walk.

The Walk

1 From the pub turn left past the village school and continue along the footpath running alongside the road. You pass an imposing, neo-Renaissance mansion on the right called Clandon Regis. This and King's Clandon are former names of the village. As West Clandon's varied architecture demonstrates, it is, indeed, a historic place. It really got itself placed on the map when the Guildford-Cobham-Waterloo railway line arrived in 1885 and has been most sought-after commuterland ever since. After about ¼ mile you reach a stile on your left.

2 At this point cross the road to a metal fingerpost leading onto an enclosed footpath. On your right you soon pass the car park and clubhouse of a golf course, also called Clandon Regis. Go over a footbridge and maintain direction straight across a golfing fairway. Continue through a gap in some trees and past some mounds on your right. As you approach a hedge and ditch, bear left towards a marker post and then continue, right, along the side of a hedge. A kissing-gate leads you onto a tree-lined path which later proceeds as a rough track, potentially muddy after wet weather. It continues through hedges and you reach a lane as you arrive at East Clandon.

3 Bear left along the lane to find an attractive pond on your left, where you bear right and shortly come out to a road. Cross the road to a bridleway slightly to your left, eventually reaching an entrance marked 'private' which leads to Fullers Farm.

Situated beyond the farm is Hatchlands Park. This handsome brick house, in the care of the National Trust, was built in the 1750s by Stiff Leadbetter for Edward Boscawen, hero of the battle of Louisberg. According to a memorial to Admiral Boscawen, in his native Cornwall, it was rebuilt at the expense of the enemies of his country. This refers to his battles with the French on the seas around Quebec (battle of Louisberg) and Porto Bello, Portugal. Apparently he seized much booty and his share contributed to the cost of having the fine mansion at Hatchlands built. The house has splendid interiors by Robert Adam. In 1988 the Cobbe collection of fine keyboard instruments, paintings and furniture was installed there and the house was extensively redecorated. To visit the house, as well as the small garden designed by Gertrude Jekyll, open 12.30 pm to 6 pm Tuesday, Wednesday, Thursday, Sunday and on bank holidays from April to October, you would need to return to the A246 and travel east to the main entrance (tel: 01483 222482).

Continuing your walk, turn right, still on a bridleway, now with a smart stone wall on the left, and shortly arrive back at the road. There's a stylish tithe barn conversion opposite and you cross the road, turning left then immediately right past the church.

East Clandon was once called Clandon Abbots and the medieval church of St Thomas of Canterbury was a stopping place for pilgrims on their

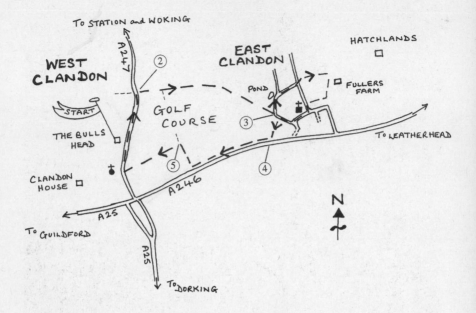

way to the county of Kent's famous city. If you want to take time out of your walk and search for interesting memorials, look for the one inside the church dedicated to Catharine Sumner who departed this earth in 1777. The family obviously considered her an extremely special person. Opposite the church is Lamp Cottage, a marvellous example of the architecture typifying this village – half-timbered and infilled with brick.

After passing the church and the village pub, the Queen's Head, turn right into Back Lane and, after about 200 yards, turn left over a stile. A veritable assault course of electric fences follows, dividing several paddocks. You finally cross another stile.

4 Turn right along a footpath running along a road, the former A246, and past some houses, noticing one with an original fence. Every conceivable garden and workshop tool has been welded together to great effect here. The old road ends and the path continues along the dual carriageway. Immediately after passing the golf club entrance, turn right onto a public footpath running along the side of a field, with the driveway over on your right, and continue to the field's end.

5 Turn left onto an enclosed path, still with the field on your left. Eventually you pass by some cottages and arrive back at The Street, with West Clandon's church, dedicated to St Peter and St Paul, opposite. This was built in the early 18th century, partially from materials from the

Church of St Thomas of Canterbury, East Clandon.

former Domesday church which was situated on the same site. Cross the road and turn right along the pavement, shortly passing the entrance to Clandon Park.

Clandon was built in the early 1730s for the 2nd Lord Onslow by the Venetian architect, Giacomo Leoni, and continued to be owned by the Onslow family for a further two centuries. This Palladian-style house, with a magnificent two-storeyed marble hall, still contains the family's pictures and furniture and the Gubbay collection of porcelain, furniture and needlework. Also of interest in this National Trust property (tel: 01483 222482) are the gardens with parterre, grotto and Maori house, and the Queen's Royal Surrey Regimental Museum. Clandon is open 1.30 pm to 5.30 pm Sunday to Wednesday from April to October and on Good Friday.

Soon after passing a footpath turning on the left you'll find yourself back at the pub.

8 Albury
The Drummond Arms

The Drummond Arms (freehouse) was originally called the Running Horse and then renamed after a local luminary, Henry Drummond, a banker and politician. In the 19th century he owned the nearby Albury Park and just about everything else around here and had the village moved from the interior of his estate to its present location. There's been a beer shop, alehouse and even a brewery on the site for a couple of centuries or more.

This smart pub comprises a spacious, comfortable lounge bar with a more recently added conservatory and a separate stylish restaurant, complete with aquarium. Outside in the garden is a large area where seating is under cover, giving shelter from the sun or the rain and wind as appropriate.

Oriental dishes are a speciality. Much of the food is cooked by the chef outside, weather permitting, using calor gas woks. A whole pig, which takes 10 hours to roast, is served every Sunday and bank holiday throughout the summer. Everything is prepared on the premises and daily changing specials may include Worcestershire pie, pork in hot bean sauce, harlequin gammon or even nasi-goreng – an Indonesian rice dish. An extensive bar menu covers the usual pub grub favourites, such as beefburgers, sandwiches, ploughman's lunches, jacket potatoes, soups, steaks, salads, and there are a number of desserts. The restaurant has its own menu with some very tempting meals. As for drinks, there's a wide choice of real ales, which regularly include King & Barnes Broadwood, Festive and Sussex, Courage Best and Directors as well as Young's Bitter. The draught cider is Dry Blackthorn and the Irish stout Beamish. A good selection of wines are available by the bottle or glass. Children under the age of 14 are not permitted in the bars but are welcome in the garden, including the covered section. They will be entertained by the ducks in their enclosed area of the stream at the far end. Dogs, as long as they are not too big or too dirty, are allowed in the bar.

The pub is open on Monday to Friday from 11 am to 2.30 pm and 6 pm to 11 pm, on Saturday from 11 am to 3 pm and 6 pm to 11 pm, and on Sunday from 12 noon to 3 pm and 7 pm to 10.30 pm. Food is served every day at lunchtime between 12 noon and 2 pm. In the evening it is available between 7 pm and 9.30 pm on Monday to Thursday and on Sunday, and from 7 pm to 10 pm on Friday and Saturday.

Telephone: 01483 202039.

How to get there: From Guildford go south on the A281 to Shalford. Turn left on the A248 and travel 3 miles, via Chilworth, to find the pub on your left as you enter the village of Albury. From the A25 Dorking to Guildford road join the A248 close to the Silent Pool and find the pub after 1 mile, on the right, soon after you enter the village.

Parking: There is a large car park which, with permission, you are welcome to use whilst on the walk.

Length of the walk: About 3 miles. OS maps: Landranger 186 Aldershot and Guildford and 187 Dorking and Reigate or Pathfinder 1226 Dorking (inn GR 048478).

You soon leave Albury with its fascinating chimneys and, after travelling through some attractive woodland, a panoramic vista of hills and woods opens out. Well concealed and blending unobtrusively into the countryside, a railway line, otherwise only revealed if a train happens along, is made apparent as you cross a long, straight section of track. A small part of one of Surrey's finest open spaces, Blackheath, is also explored.

The Walk

1   From the pub cross the road and turn left along the pavement, passing a building with some very tall and most ornate Tudor-style chimneys. These were designed by Pugin, as was most of the village and, if you look carefully, you'll notice that no pair is alike. After the last building on the left turn right through an easily-missed metal barrier onto an enclosed,

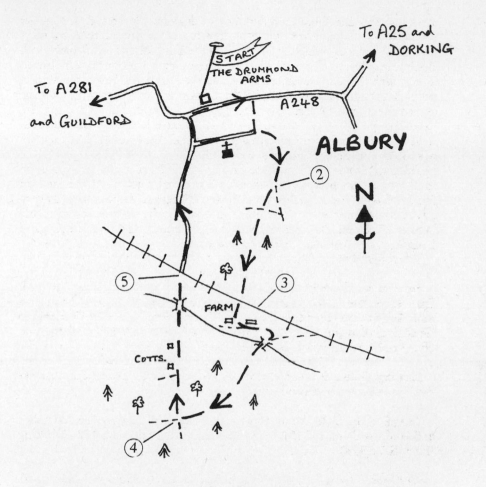

tarred footpath. At the top of the slope turn left onto a track, which later bears right into a gully with many exposed tree roots. After passing gates either side of the track, continue for a few more yards up the slope to a waymarked post.

2 From the bridleway bear right onto a footpath leading you into the woodland of Albury Warren. At the top of another slope go over a crossing track, passing redundant stiles on both sides. Continue into a pine plantation and, as you emerge from the trees, cross a stile into a large field. Turn left onto a beaten track taking you across the field. As you continue downwards you should be enjoying good views on a fine day. Pass some magnificent oak trees on your right and soon reach a gate by a railway line. Cross the track and go forward to the nearest row of trees.

Continue between the trees then go through a gate and alongside a half-timbered cottage. Another gate leads you to a farm track.

3   Bear left onto the track, passing some farm buildings and a wooden house. The track curves left and right and on your right you will notice some former watercress beds, now sadly neglected. You reach a T-junction and turn right onto a track, immediately crossing one of the streams feeding the Tillingbourne, which all meet at Shere. Enter a canopy of trees leading you onto Blackheath. After about ¼ mile reach a fingerpost and continue ahead on bridleway 237. Ignore an enticing little uphill path on your right and keep to the main bridleway, shortly reaching an open area and a junction of several tracks.

4   Bear right on the main track, passing two paths leading off to the right, and keep left of a waymarked post. Your path becomes bracken-lined and sunken in bright yellow sand as you descend past a Hurtwood Control notice to reach a junction where another path comes in from the left. Keep right, passing a cottage, The Hame, and your track becomes tarred as you pass Barton Cottage. Via a small bridge go over the same stream you crossed earlier and, after passing a gate on your right and a footpath turning on the left, continue under the railway.

5   You join Blackheath Lane, which looks as if it was at one time a watercourse that cut deeply into the rock on either side. At the top of a slope a wide track comes in from the right and you maintain direction ahead. Look to your left for some good views across the fields and then pass a large barn. If you go a few yards up a slope towards a gate you'll enjoy excellent views across the fields towards Albury with its church and the North Downs beyond. At the end of the lane you reach a road junction and turn right. A couple of hundred yards along the road, past a pretty cottage, Betswy, and the local bowls club, you will reach the church.

Erected in the middle of the 19th century by Henry Drummond, this church is, unusually, built of red brick rather than the more customary stone and is in the style of one located in Thaon in Normandy.

Having seen the church, retrace your steps down the road, bearing right to the main road and the pub.

9 Shere
The Prince of Wales

The Prince of Wales (Labatt's) has a typically Victorian feel, both inside and out, and looks down from its elevated position over the pretty village of Shere, one of the most picturesque in Surrey. Whereas many of the buildings in the vicinity date from the 1600s, this particular one only goes back a century and a half or so.

In 1995 the pub changed allegiance to a Canadian company and was extensively refurbished. The result is a smart, roomy house with modern facilities yet recapturing something of the rural atmosphere of bygone times. Many agricultural implements, including sieves, spades, forks, yokes and even part of a hay cart, decorate the walls and ceiling, adding to the pleasant ambience. There are plenty of tables and chairs around the two large bars with their polished wood and flagstone floors, partially carpeted. The adjacent dining area provides comfortable seating for non-smokers. There is also a separate function room available by advance booking for parties, including walking groups. For warmer days there is seating outside on a grassy area.

A good proportion of the food is home-prepared and everything available is displayed on the blackboards. The comprehensive menu runs the whole gamut from sandwiches to steaks, and special requirements are catered for wherever possible. Indian cuisine is featured, with complete menus at an all-inclusive price and the home-made curries are also available as take-aways. The four regular real ales are Boddingtons, Theakston, Tanglefoot and Flowers IPA and there is a frequently changing guest ale. Draught Guinness and Strongbow cider are also available. Children are welcome inside as long as they are kept away from the bar. Dogs, however, are not permitted inside the pub.

The pub is open on Monday to Saturday from 11 am to 11 pm, and on Sunday from 12 noon to 10.30 pm. Food is served every day from 12 noon to 3 pm, and in the evening on Sunday to Wednesday from 6 pm to 9 pm, and on Thursday to Saturday from 6 pm to 10 pm.

Telephone: 01483 202313.

How to get there: Leave the A25 between Guildford and Dorking, at either of the two signs for Shere. Turn into the village main street (Middle Street) and the pub is found on the right at the far end.

Parking: Shere is a busy village, particularly at weekends, and parking is at a premium, so please seek permission before leaving your car in the pub's car park whilst on the walk. If there are problems you should find additional parking in the recreation ground at the other end of Middle Street.

Length of the walk: About 3 miles. OS maps: Landranger 187 Dorking and Reigate or Pathfinder 1226 Dorking (inn GR 073477).

In an area rich in history, this is a pleasant walk, starting and finishing in one of the loveliest villages of Surrey's heartland. You soon leave the bustle of the streets to discover peaceful paths running through a secluded country estate and leading to an ancient, disused, but still accessible, church.

The Walk

1   From the pub turn left into the centre of Shere. Take the turning on the right opposite the village's other pub, the White Horse Inn, and, in a few yards, arrive at St James's church.

The church is a fine example of mainly early English ecclesiastical architecture, and some of its walls are Norman, or even earlier. The tower is Norman and the spire, with its excellent shingle work, is still supported by 14th-century oak timbers. The lychgate leading to the churchyard was designed by Sir Edwin Lutyens.

Retrace your steps to Middle Street and take the turning opposite, Lower Street. The lane runs along the side of the Tillingbourne, which is fed by four tributaries rising from different places – Peaslake, Holmbury St Mary, Abinger Bottom and Leith Hill. From Shere the river continues

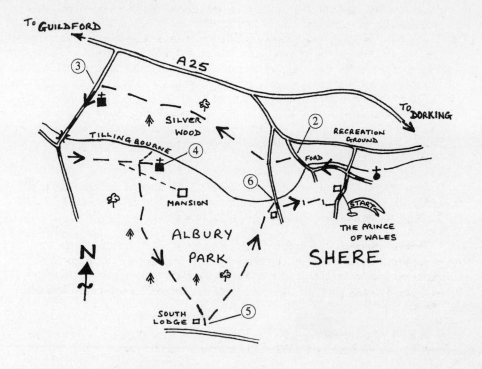

its course through Shalford and into the Wey.

You pass some fine old buildings, including the Old Forge and the Old Pumphouse opposite. A little further along is a flint and brick building with an overhanging upper storey and barred window, a former lock-up. When you reach a junction, turn right on Rectory Lane. Cross a ford and in about 100 yards, at the top of a slope, you come to a footpath on the left.

2 Fork left onto the enclosed footpath and later cross a lane to a sloping footpath leading to a field. Continue straight across, noticing a walled garden on the left belonging to the Albury Estate. You go through a gate into the attractive Silver Wood and eventually your path dips down to a stile by a gate, where you leave the wood to continue over a narrow, fenced strip of land. As the fence ends, continue across the field, going over another stile onto a track and down to a road.

3 Turn left along the footpath and, in a few yards, you reach one of the first churches of the Catholic Apostolic Movement.

This church was built by Henry Drummond for £15,000 in 1840. The banker and politician gave it to his friend Edward Irving, the founder of a new and colourful Christian sect. There are few Irvingites left today and the spectacular church has long been closed. However, if you want to see the fine woodwork and tilework at close hand the keys may be obtained from the caretaker living in a nearby cottage.

Continue along the footpath, later recrossing the Tillingbourne via a bridge, and turn left into New Road. Turn left again onto the driveway leading to Albury Park, a private residence open to the public from May to September on Wednesday and Thursday afternoons. Continue on the driveway, lined with beautiful oak, beech and chestnut trees, which gives access to the church of St Peter and St Paul. When the driveway forks, keep left and as it curves left to The Bothy, continue straight ahead over the grass to the church. A notice at the door gives the opening times.

This isolated Norman church stands on Saxon foundations. Around 1140 the tower was built over the original chancel and there have been many further additions over the centuries. The former manorial chapel was remodelled by Pugin as a mortuary chapel for the Drummond family. If you are able to go inside the church, look for the 15th-century wall painting of St Christopher. There is a range of information for sale, telling you about the church, the estate and the magnificent trees found here.

4   From the church retrace your steps but, just before reaching the tarred driveway, turn left on a grassy track and go over the driveway leading to the mansion. Continue up a slope and go through a gate to join a footpath running through enclosed woodland. Your track twists and turns for about ½ mile and you should ignore all turnings and crossing tracks, following the waymarks at all junctions, where you are reminded that you are going over private land. The attractive mossy path winds through plantations, offering delightful views across to the North Downs. Finally it curves left to a T-junction. Turn right, soon passing a cottage, South Lodge, and come out to a road via a gate.

5   Turn sharply left through a kissing-gate onto a wide grassy path running between fences and wonderful lines of horse chestnut trees. Pass a redundant stile, continue towards a house and go through a gate. Turn sharply right for only a few paces and, just before reaching the house, find a stile on the left.

6   Cross the stile into a field, go through a gate and pass along the side of a cemetery, with another path and the Tillingbourne running parallel down on your left. You reach a gate, turn right and immediately left through another, then pass between houses. Turn right and swing left again to arrive at a road which, for safety, you should cross to the pavement opposite. Turn left past Shere museum and shortly arrive back at the pub.

10 West Horsley
The King William IV

The King William IV (Courage), or 'Ye Olde King Billy' as it is affectionately known by locals, is an attractive pub both inside and out. The building dates from about 250 years ago when it formed two gamekeepers' cottages. An interesting feature is the coffin windows – these were installed to enable coffins to be removed from the building without the indignity of attempting to squeeze the long boxes around narrow staircases.

The pub comprises a public bar, complete with darts, pool table, juke box and fruit machines, and, for those seeking a more relaxed atmosphere, an attractive L-shaped bar with tables and comfortable chairs. Leading off is a servery and another dining area suitable for families with children. A fairly recent addition to the pub is a restaurant seating 50. The ceiling timbers are not as ancient as they look but these products of the 1987 hurricane, installed when the pub was being renovated, give the place the feel of a traditional country inn. There's a garden at the rear where barbecues are held in fine weather.

The landlord prides himself on the quality of the food, virtually all of which is home-prepared. A bar menu and a specials blackboard list the numerous choices and for the evening there is an à la carte menu. You are welcome to have anything you fancy from these menus regardless of where you sit – bar or restaurant. The options will usually include home-made soups, steak and kidney pie, liver and bacon, cheese and broccoli quiche and cold beef salad, in addition to all the usual pub grub. The real ales are Courage Best, King & Barnes Sussex and Wadworth 6X. For cider drinkers there is Dry Blackthorn and Cidermaster and the Irish stout is Guinness. A red, a medium white and a dry white wine are served by the glass. Children are welcome in the family area and dogs in the public bar.

The pub is open on Monday to Friday from 11 am to 3 pm and 6 pm to 11 pm, on Saturday from 11 am to 4 pm and 6 pm to 11 pm, and on Sunday from 12 noon to 3 pm and 7 pm to 10.30 pm. Food is served every day from 12 noon to 2.30 pm, and on Tuesday to Saturday from 7 pm to 9.30 pm. No food is available on Sunday and Monday evenings.

Telephone: 01483 282318.

How to get there: West Horsley is just north of the A246 Guildford to Leatherhead road. Turning at the roundabout by the Bell and Colvill garage, take the road signposted to Ripley (The Street) and continue for about ½ mile to find the pub on the left. Horsley railway station is about ½ mile from Point 3.

Parking: The pub has a car park which you are welcome to use, with permission, whilst on your walk. Alternatively, there is a good car park behind West Horsley church, from where you could commence the walk at Point 6.

Length of the walk: About 5 miles, which can be reduced to about 3 miles. OS maps: Landranger 187 Dorking and Reigate or Pathfinder 1206 Woking and Leatherhead (inn GR 078529).

This walk embraces two differing terrains – the farmland north of the busy A246 and, to the south, Sheepleas, one of Surrey's most-loved Open Spaces in the care of the County Council. You are permitted to wander at will on all the paths over this vast tract of countryside, and if you only used the rights of ways shown on the OS map you might well miss the attractive meadows, with their diversity of flora, discovered on this walk. It's possible to take a shorter route or even do the walk in two parts – but try to explore Sheepleas if you possibly can.

The Walk

1 From the pub cross the road and turn right along the pavement for a few yards, then you turn left on School Lane. At the end cross another road, Mount Pleasant, and continue on an enclosed footpath. You reach some houses and a cattery and turn right and immediately left, soon crossing a stile on the right. Continue over a field, firstly with a fence on

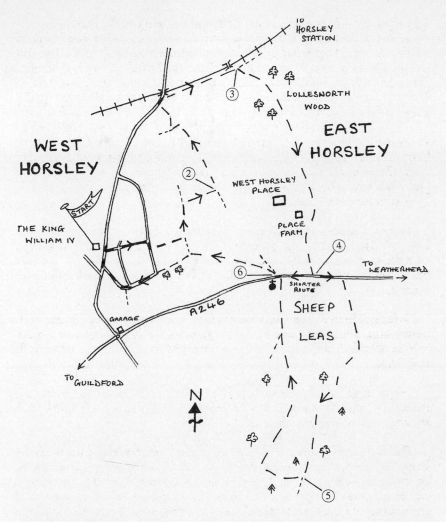

your left, and reach a T-junction. Turn left and halfway along this large field turn right on a path running between fields and leading to another T-junction.

2 Turn left and continue along the edge of the large field, with a hedge on your right. At the far end go through a line of trees and turn left, then right along another field towards a railway embankment. Go over a stile, then soon over another and out to a road, which you cross to the pavement opposite. Turn right for a few yards and, just before a bridge, turn right across the road to take a tarred path, running parallel with the railway, for about ¼ mile.

3 Pass a bridge over the railway and almost immediately turn right, shortly entering Lollesworth Wood. You pass a gate and enter a large field. At the end of the field the path becomes enclosed in trees and bears right towards the buildings of Place Farm. Keep to the left of a barn and continue on the farm track ahead down to the A246.

For the shorter route, turn right along the pavement to West Horsley church and continue from Point 6.

To complete the full route, taking in the best part of the walk – Sheepleas:
4 Turn left along the pavement for about 200 yards and cross the road to the West Horsley sign opposite, joining a bridleway and shortly going through a gateway into Sheepleas. Keep to the main track for about ½ mile and when you reach a fork take either branch, although the left one avoids any mud after wet weather. You pass a left and a right turn and in a few yards, at a crossing track, go left on the bridleway to reach a junction of paths where you continue ahead. Shortly you reach another path junction and take the second path, going diagonally left, almost continuing in the same direction. Upon reaching an open area, with a large dead tree on the left, stop and look back at the panoramic view. In a few more yards you come to a fork.
5 Fork right along a grassy track and shortly you are led over a crossing track, through a barrier and out to a well-defined track on which you bear left. You arrive at a T-junction by a white-banded post and turn right on the bridleway. In another 50 yards you reach a crossing track just beyond a tree-stump seat. Turn right towards a green-banded post and find yourself in a pleasant open area dotted with picnic tables and seats. At a crossing track turn right and, after about 100 yards, fork left through a barrier to arrive in a beautiful meadow covered, in season, with thousands of wild flowers.

The flora in this area, and in the meadows you are about to pass through, is a wonderful sight. In spring cowslips abound and in summer you will find thyme as well as the ubiquitous rosebay willowherb. There are also many more species to detect. Surrey County Council (SCC) wish to remind us that, although the wild flowers are seemingly abundant, some have been close to extinction due to excessive picking. The numbers have increased and will continue to do so as long as they are not picked. Please leave them for others to enjoy and also for the wildlife that depends upon them.

Continue ahead and pass another green-banded post and, at a fork, keep right on the wider, uphill, path. Go through a barrier and eventually arrive at a bridleway fingerpost. Follow the track signposted to St Mary's car park and soon fork left through a barrier marked with a green band. You pass a handsome seat constructed at the SCC sawmills in Norbury Park near Leatherhead. You walk through one fine meadow followed by yet another, in a mainly north-westerly direction, passing a seat complete with

West Horsley church.

canopy to keep off the sun or the rain as the case may be. Go under a barrier and onto a bridleway, keeping ahead towards a roadway serving a car park over to your left. You then come to a church.

West Horsley church has a most interesting history. Perhaps its greatest claim to fame is that the head of the executed knight, Walter Raleigh, is supposed to be buried in a vault in the south chapel. Apparently his widow, who lived opposite the church in West Horsley Place, preserved it in a red leather bag for 25 years and then buried it with one of his sons.

Cross the A246 and turn left for a few yards to a stile.

6   Cross over the stile and look to your right at the grand mansion.

West Horsley Place is now the home of the Dowager Duchess of Roxburghe, owner of much of the land in these parts. Over the centuries, no less than three of the house's former owners, including the Marquis of Exeter in 1538, lost their heads on the executioner's block, just like Sir Walter.

Continue diagonally left on a path running across a large field and at the far side go through a snatch of trees. Bear left along the edge of a field, with a wood on your left. Later bear left onto a track which leads you to a residential road. You pass a turning on the right, Mount Pleasant, which you crossed at the beginning of the walk and the road then curves right, bringing you out to a main road with The Old Rectory opposite. Turn right along the pavement, shortly arriving back at the pub.

good for hids
aggressive ducks
in the beer garden

11 Abinger Common
The Abinger Hatch

The Abinger Hatch (freehouse) has been an inn since the 17th century. Between the two World Wars the two Hatches (the other is Wotton Hatch) were managed by the Surrey Trust, which aimed to reduce 'excessive drinking by the working classes'. The landlords received no commission on the sale of ale but supplemented their income by taking in guests. Regulars here were Elsie and Doris Waters of 'Gert and Daisy' fame. Charabanc parties, hikers and ramblers were also encouraged.

The bar is on two levels, the lower with its original flagstone floor. The rustic seating comprises chairs and wooden benches, some of which are padded, and in winter there's a real fire to welcome you. In the evening a separate restaurant opens. Wednesday evening is music night and this can be jazz, rock or folk – sometimes a group and other times a solo artist.

Almost all the food, and there's a good variety, is home-prepared. The choices are displayed on the board but if you are looking for something else, a sandwich for example, it will be made for you, if at all possible. The steak and Guinness pie and curries are particularly recommended and there are also salads, home-made soup, basket meals, lasagne and so on. Children's portions are available. Evening diners using the restaurant will be offered the 'Country Table' table d'hôte menu listing five starters, six main courses and four sweets. Real ale devotees are spoilt for choice, with

Hogs Back TEA and APB, Badger Best, Wadworth 6X, Ringwood Fortyniner and Tanglewood. The draught ciders are Dry Blackthorn and a pretty deadly scrumpy, and Guinness also comes through a tap. Wines by the glass are available, too. Children are welcome in the pub, as are well-behaved dogs. Outside, there's an attractive beer garden and children's amusements are installed in summer.

The pub is open on Monday to Saturday from 11 am to 2.30 pm and 6 pm to 11 pm, and on Sunday from 12 noon to 3 pm and 7 pm to 10.30 pm. Food is served at lunchtime from 12 noon to 2 pm (2.30 pm on Sunday). It is also available in the evenings from Tuesday to Saturday, between 7 pm and 10 pm.

Telephone: 01306 730737.

How to get there: Abinger Common lies to the south of the A25 Guildford to Dorking road. Leave the A25 between Abinger Hammer and Wotton, travelling south on the road signposted to Abinger Common, Leith Hill and Friday Street. In a little less than a mile take a narrow turning on the right and at the ensuing T-junction turn right to find the pub on your immediate right, opposite the church.

Parking: There is parking in front of and behind the pub, which you may use whilst on your walk, but you should check with the landlord first.

Length of the walk: About 2¾ miles and this may be reduced to 2 miles if required. OS maps: Landranger 187 Dorking and Reigate or Pathfinder 1226 Dorking (inn GR 116459).

This short walk takes you through part of the vast Wotton Estate and visits Holmbury St Mary with its magnificent sandstone church. The return journey through Pasture Wood affords a pleasant view across to the Downs.

The Walk

1   From the pub cross the road to the small green opposite. On the right are the remains of the village stocks – it is professed that they were never used. In a field nearby are the remains of a Mesolithic pit dwelling, giving Abinger Common the claim to be one of the oldest settlements in England.

Continue through the lychgate into the churchyard of St James, patron saint of pilgrims. This is quite appropriate as the Pilgrims' Way, running from Winchester to Canterbury, passes a little to the north of here. The church, which took the full force of a flying bomb blast in 1944, was restored in 1950 only to be severely damaged again by a fire in 1964, this

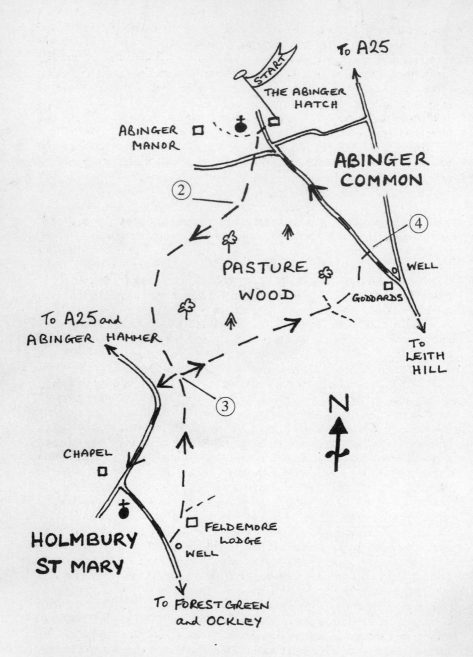

START

THE ABINGER HATCH

To A25

ABINGER MANOR

ABINGER COMMON

②

PASTURE WOOD

④

WELL

GODDARDS

To A25 and ABINGER HAMMER

③

To LEITH HILL

N

CHAPEL

HOLMBURY ST MARY

FELDEMORE LODGE

Well

To FOREST GREEN and OCKLEY

time caused by lightning.

Pass through the churchyard (the war memorial was designed by Lutyens) and on the other side look for an impressive motte which surrounded the former manor house. Retrace your steps to the lychgate, where you should turn right alongside the churchyard wall. Pass by an attractive enclosed play area for the village children and cross a lane to some steps and a stile opposite. Continue straight across a large field and enter the woods on the other side via another stile.

2   After just a few yards ignore an opening on the right and immediately turn right onto a narrow path, the entrance to which may possibly be obscured. Shortly go under cables and reach a T-junction where you turn right. Later you pass a wide turning on the left and continue ahead with a wire fence on your left. The heather-lined path widens and you pass a small housing estate over on your right, one garden enclosed by an ornate wall. Your track curves round to the left and you go over a stile by a gate, passing a notice indicating that you have just left the Wotton Estate. In a few yards find another stile on your left. Here you have a choice.

For the shorter walk, go over the stile and continue from Point 3.

For the main walk, taking in Holmbury St Mary and its elevated and imposing church and pretty village pump, turn right on a wide track. If you look to your left, you will see a rather neglected swimming pool, complete with derelict changing rooms, formed by the damming of the stream, one of the Tillingbourne tributaries. Shortly reach the B2126 and turn left along a footpath, passing houses on the edge of the village of Holmbury St Mary. Soon, if you look across to the right, you'll see Felday Chapel and, as the road curves left, come upon the church occupying its impressive hillside position amidst pine trees.

Dedicated to St Mary the Virgin, the church was designed and erected in 1879 by George Edward Street, who had built a house, Holmdale, in the village. Constructed of local stone with Bath stone dressings, the church was his last professional work and was given to the parish in memory of his second wife. Prime Minister Gladstone and the cabinet visited G. E. Street's home in 1880. Such was his reputation (his London designs included the Law Courts) that he was buried in Westminster Abbey.

Continue along the road and soon reach the village pump with its thatched roof, where you turn left on a bridleway and go through a small wooden gate by a house, Feldemore Lodge. Shortly, reach a fork by an old wooden shed, where you keep left and continue past the gardens of the houses you saw earlier. You return to the garden with the derelict swimming pool and go over the stile on the right.

3   Having crossed the stile, climb the steep slope. At the top is a pleasant, wide grassy track taking you over Pasture Wood. Later you pass a wide opening on the left offering excellent views across to the North Downs. Eventually you are led down to a crossing track and continue ahead to a

Village pump and well, Abinger Common.

fence. Bear left on a path going between fences which later becomes more enclosed and brings you out to a road.

4   Cross the road and turn right along a green to see the imposing, well-preserved village pump and well, complete with machinery, built over 100 years ago by William John Evelyn, Lord of the Manor of Abinger. The Lutyens-designed house opposite, Goddards, was built originally as a rest house for 'ladies of small means'.

To resume the walk retrace your steps along the green and continue through the village of Abinger Common and back to the pub.

12 Westcott
The Crown Inn

The Crown Inn (Pubmaster) has parts going back to 1450, when King Henry VI was on the throne but the frontage is Georgian, dating from 1812. The building has always been a hostelry and at one time provided stabling for the extra horses required to haul especially heavy carts and carriages up nearby Coast Hill.

At one end of the semi-circular bar is the games area with dartboard and pool table. Tables for dining surround the central area and at the other end are a piano and horse-riding pictures and trophies. Saddles and other horsey memorabilia reflect the landlord's passion for all things equestrian. As soon as the weather cools the inn is heated by a glowing real log fire.

Meals here range from the very light to the extremely naughty. Those denied a 'fry-up' at home will be offered sympathy and greatly tempted by some of the fare. Among the specials you will usually find a home-made soup and dishes such as chilli con carne and steak and kidney pie. There's always a curry, plus a vegetable one, home-cooked ham and fried (fresh) fish, perhaps '*proper* battered cod and chips'. If your meal includes a roll it will have been baked on the premises that morning. Having eaten, you could then relax with your choice of four different coffees, served in cafetières or, most unusual for a pub, one of six different teas, including herbal. All the real ales change periodically but on our visit Boddingtons,

Bass, Hancocks and Wethered's Royal were on offer as were both Guinness and Caffrey's Irish Ale. The cider is Addlestone's and wine is served by the glass. In winter you could try the mulled wine. Children, as long as they are well-behaved, are allowed in the pub. So, normally, are dogs, but please check with the landlord before bringing them in. There is a small garden at the rear.

The pub is open on Monday to Thursday from 11 am to 3.30 pm and 5.30 pm to 11 pm, on Friday and Saturday from 11 am to 11 pm, and on Sunday from 12 noon to 4 pm and 6 pm to 10.30 pm. Food is served on Monday to Saturday from 12 noon to 2.30 pm and 7 pm to 9.45 pm, and on Sunday from 12 noon to 2.30 pm and 7 pm to 9.30 pm.

Telephone: 01306 885414.

How to get there: Westcott is on the A25 about 2 miles to the west of Dorking, and the pub's sign is easily spotted. If coming from Dorking you should look carefully for the pub on the left, shortly after entering the village. If you are approaching from the Guildford direction, look out for the triangular green on the left and find the pub some 200 yards beyond it on the right.

Parking: There is small car park, which you are welcome to use whilst on the walk, but seek permission first.

Length of the walk: About 2½ miles. OS maps: Landranger 187 Dorking and Reigate or Pathfinder 1226 Dorking (inn GR 144486).

Westcott is a pleasant village which you may wish to explore further. This is horse country and from the village you are led past a succession of paddocks before arriving in more open countryside with delightful views. Your return route takes you past a large man-made lake where anglers patiently await a bite. You also go along part of the very pretty Milton Street, following the course of a stream, where a series of bridges lead to attractive houses.

The Walk
1   From the pub turn left along the road for about ¼ mile, passing another pub, the Prince of Wales, on the opposite side. When you reach the triangular green, complete with thatched dovecote and thatched bus shelter, turn left up Parsonage Lane. At the top of the lane turn right through a barrier onto a footpath, part of the Greensand Way, and in a few yards you'll see another barrier on your left.
2   Turn left on the footpath, passing between garden fences, and you reach another barrier. Continue across a small road and alongside a succession of paddocks. Although you continue to walk between fences

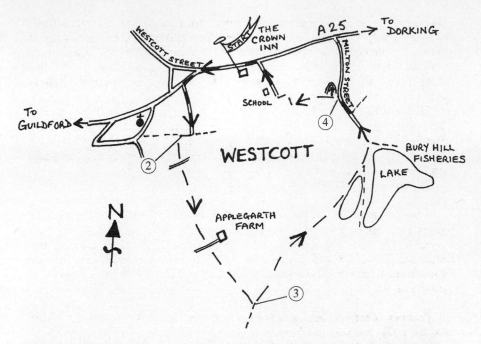

the views begin to open out. Cross a lane leading to Applegarth Farm on your left and continue ahead on the path into more open countryside. Later, if you look over to your left, you should be able to spot Old Bury House and The Observatory, on the edge of the Nower, and the spire of Ranmore church on the horizon. Shortly, at a farm gate you reach a point where your path merges with another coming in from the left.

3 Turn sharply left on the path and eventually go over a sleeper bridge and then a stile taking you into a field. Cross the field by following the fence on your right and go over another stile, formed with logs, into the next field. Continue diagonally left towards a gate at the edge of the trees ahead. In the corner you'll find a sleeper bridge leading to a stile, which you cross onto an enclosed footpath. Turn left along the perimeter of Bury Hill Fisheries and eventually cross a wooden footbridge leading to a roadway, on which you turn left. Go through a metal kissing-gate and pass the entrance to Bury Lake, popular with anglers. Continue ahead on the road, Milton Street, passing a bridleway forking right, and reach a beautiful willow tree.

4 Turn left over a bridge, back onto the Greensand Way once again, on a path running between gardens, and when you reach a gap in the fences turn right on a narrow path. This path turns left and right, leading onto a road going past a school and down to the A25. Turn left on a raised pavement which takes you back to the pub.

Westcott village.

Away from the main road, this attractive village has a peaceful character and deserves closer inspection. On the walk you've already seen the village green and dovecote but if you go back there and turn right into a narrow lane, Westcott Street, you'll find a considerable variety of architectural styles.

Further ahead on the left, high off the main road, is Holy Trinity church, designed by Sir George Gilbert Scott and opened in 1852 when Westcott became an ecclesiastical parish separate from Dorking.

13 Mickleham
The Running Horses

The Running Horses (Ind Coope) was formerly called the Chequers and has been a tavern from around 1600. It changed its name following the result of the Derby of 1828, a dead heat between Cadland and The Colonel. The two rivals are shown on one side of the sign and it is said that the winner of the subsequent re-run, Cadland, has his portrait on the other. The villagers were most proud that he had been stabled here and celebrated again when Blair Athol, who was also quartered here, won the Derby in 1864. Horsemen of another persuasion frequented the pub, too, and highwaymen's hideaways have been discovered.

This large house has considerable charm. Each of the bars has its own distinctive character and the Cadland displays a real log fire in its inglenook fireplace, which in winter months is lit. There is also seating outside at the front of the pub. An extensive menu lists the usual favourites, from soups and sandwiches right through to gourmet dishes. Everything, apart from one or two of the desserts, is home-prepared, with pies and pastries a speciality. There is a choice of six real ales, including Friary, Young's and Wadworth 6X, in addition to the house's own Cadland and two changing guest ales. Draught Guinness and Dry Blackthorn and Cidermaster ciders are also available, as well as at least six red and six white wines by the glass. Children with adults are permitted in the dining areas but not in the bars and dogs are permitted in the bars but not in the dining areas.

Telephone: 01372 372279.

How to get there: Some 2 miles south of Leatherhead or 2 miles north of Dorking leave the A24 Mickleham bypass on the road signposted to the village. The pub is a little way up the village street, opposite the church.

Parking: The pub does not have a car park but there is usually plenty of room for parking in the side street, or along the road in front, where there are no restrictions.

Length of the walk: About 3½ miles. OS maps: Landranger 187 Dorking and Reigate or Pathfinder 1206 Woking and Leatherhead (inn GR 170534).

This walk takes you over Norbury Park, reputedly one of the finest in Surrey. You're led onto many paths not shown on OS maps and these contribute to a pleasing and varied route with some very fine views.

The Walk

1 From the pub cross the road and enter the churchyard. St Michael's church dates from Saxon times, although the porch is Norman. However, the building you see today is largely of Victorian influence. Canadians visiting it will find something of particular interest – in the Norbury Chapel the late Lord Beaverbrook installed a window commemorating his two nephews who were killed in the Second World War. There is a gravestone in the churchyard in memory of Douglas Gilmour, an early air ace, infamous for his low flight over the Henley Regatta. His other claim to fame is to have been recorded as the first man killed in flight when, in 1912, he crashed to his death in Richmond Park.

Continue along the side of the churchyard wall and turn left on an enclosed footpath. Cross over a lane, continuing straight ahead to the A24 dual carriageway. Having crossed the road with care, go left for a few yards, then turn right onto a bridge taking you over the river Mole.

The river dries up and goes underground in very hot spells, which endorses the intrepid traveller Celia Fiennes' remark, in about 1700, that 'just about Dorken and Leatherhead it sinkes away in many places which they call swallow holes'.

2 You join the driveway leading into Norbury Park and continue along this for about 50 yards.

After changing hands with considerable frequency, most of the park was finally acquired, for public enjoyment, by Surrey County Council in the mid-1930s and thus saved from being carved up into building plots.

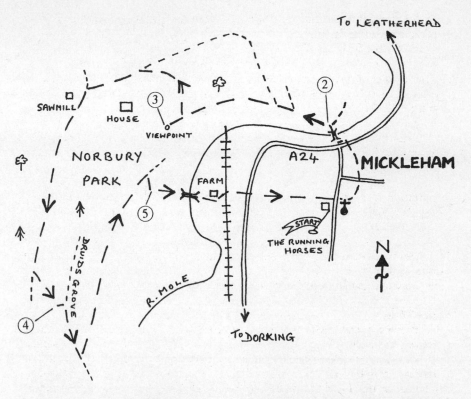

Turn left off the driveway onto an enclosed bridleway. You pass a turning to the left and continue up the slope, eventually rejoining the winding driveway you left earlier. Shortly, the drive divides and you take the left fork, passing a seat on your right. Pass another footpath turning on the left and, where the drive curves to the right, keep straight ahead on a path, still climbing uphill. The track continues through woodland and you reach a turning on the left, signposted to a viewpoint. Turn left to take in the wonderful view of Mickleham Downs ahead of you. Box Hill, obscured from view, is just beyond. Over to the right is the south-east's highest point, Leith Hill.

3   From the viewpoint retrace your steps to the signpost and now turn left. Shortly, pass some gates leading to the rear entrance of Norbury Park House and continue round to the left, following the fence back to the driveway. Turn left to arrive at the main gate to the house.

Norbury Park House, built in 1774, was once the home of the birth control advocate Dr Marie Stopes. It is famous for its 'painted room' with walls and ceilings decorated with landscapes which dovetail into the views from the windows. The house was for some time also in the ownership of

Surrey County Council but is now a sumptuous private residence.

Continue up the drive to a junction where you bear left, keeping to the fence and soon going past the County Council's sawmill on the right. You go through a barrier and, when the fence on the left ends, continue straight ahead on a fine tarred track. A signpost points the way to another magnificent view, only a few yards away, which you may like to see and then return to the tarred track. Later a bridleway comes in from the right, and shortly another forks to the right, but you stay on the tarred track as it curves left and goes downhill for another 100 yards. Here you'll find a fingerpost pointing to 'Druids Grove'.

4   Turn left down some steps, arrive at a T-junction and turn right along Druids Grove, a narrow path lined with yew trees. Watch out for roots and holes in the path, which later curves left down to a T-junction where you turn left onto a wider track. Remain on this pleasant path, often with fine views over the fields on the right, for about ½ mile then turn sharply right on a signposted footpath leading to a gate and stile onto Swanworth picnic site. Leave the picnic site via another gate opposite and arrive at a three-way fingerpost.

5   Turn left on a fenced track, back over the river Mole, and head towards farm buildings, which you pass by turning right then left. You leave the farmyard and cross the railway.

Although you may not have realised it, you crossed the railway, which was in a long, deep tunnel, earlier in the walk whilst in Norbury Park. The line and its tunnel entrances caused quite a furore when they were first mooted. John Stuart Mill, the famous philosopher-economist – and local resident – strenuously protested. He failed to stop the railway but subsequently became a founder of the Commons Preservation Society, which is now known as the Open Spaces Society.

You arrive back at the A24, which you again cross with care, to the footpath opposite. Continue on this wide path, with playing fields each side, back to the pub.

14 Blackbrook
The Plough at Blackbrook

The Plough (King & Barnes) is a popular, busy pub. It's been an inn for a couple of centuries or more, with parts of the building dating from over 400 years ago. The main part is Georgian and the frontage, with a riot of colourful flowers in summer, has a definite Victorian look about it. Upstairs there's a priest-hole where persecuted Roman Catholics once hid.

On entering the front door, turn left if you are looking for a dining room and bar. Alternatively, turn right if you are seeking a more traditional country inn atmosphere. On the far wall is the largest collection of company, regimental and school ties you have ever seen. There are over 700 of them. And if you are planning to eat, there's a cosy dining area leading from here, too. Old sewing machines are put to good use as tables and woodsaws from yesteryear decorate the ceiling.

Very many of the pub's clientele come here to eat since this pub has received many awards for its food, most of which is home-prepared. The specials board, changed every two weeks, has starters, main courses such as 'grilled Wiltshire gammon with peaches and everything', and puddings. The regular bar menu has walkers' favourites like ploughman's lunches, snacks including taramasalata or houmous with salad garnish and toast, basket meals with chips and salad, filled jacket potatoes and many substantial meals. All of the real ales come from King & Barnes' Horsham brewery in barrels marked Sussex, Broadwood and Festive. This popular threesome is supplemented with a seasonal bitter such as Harvest Ale or Winter Warmer. Something you won't find in many pubs these days, mild ale, is also on offer. The draught Irish stout is Guinness and Stowford Press cider is also on tap. Traditional country wine lovers are spoilt for choice with no less than 20. The blackboard warns you they are 'Very warming, strong and potent. Drink with care!' A large range of wines is also available by the glass. Children under 14 are not allowed inside and dogs on leads are only permitted in the Blackbrook bar. Behind the pub there's a pleasant beer garden with a Wendy House for younger children.

The opening times on Monday to Friday are from 11 am to 2.30 pm and 6 pm to 11 pm, on Saturday from 11 am to 3 pm and 6 pm to 11 pm, and on Sunday from 12 noon to 3 pm and 7 pm to 10.30 pm. Food is available every day from 12 noon to 2 pm and 7 pm to 9.30 pm, apart from Monday when no food is served in the evening.

Telephone: 01306 886603.

How to get there: From the roundabout at the A24/A25 intersection east of Dorking go south on the A24 for about a mile, where you take a left turn on a road signposted to Blackbrook. In about ½ mile pass a pub on your right and about a mile further on you will find the Plough at a bend on the left. If travelling north, leave the A24 at South Holmwood, turning right into Mill Road, signposted to Leigh and Brockham. In a little less than a mile you reach a T-junction and a pond, where you turn left. About a mile further on you will find the pub on the right, soon after the second of two right turnings.

Parking: If the pub is not too busy you will be welcome to park there whilst on the walk, but please seek permission first. Alternatively, start the walk from the car park at Fourwents Pond (Point 5) and visit the pub halfway round the walk.

Length of the walk: About 3 miles. OS maps: Landranger 187 Dorking and Reigate or Pathfinder 1226 Dorking (inn GR 181467).

Close to one of the county's best-loved towns, Dorking, this entire walk is on the vast expanse of Holmwood Common, now in the care of the National Trust. Just across the road from the pub is a quiet and virtually unspoilt piece of open space, criss-crossed by a network of footpaths and bridleways. A gentle climb rewards you with a grandstand view of the surrounding area. Partway through the walk you arrive at a large expanse of water, the attractive Fourwents Pond.

The Walk

1 From the pub cross the road with care to join the public footpath opposite, taking you into the woods of Holmwood Common and following Black Brook down on your right. After about ¼ mile you pass a post on your left, with blue (bridleway) and yellow (footpath) arrows, and continue ahead, keeping to the edge of the wood with its profusion of oak and holly. Ignore a turning on the left, continuing ahead on the main path and passing an attractive garden over on your right. Eventually you go over a footbridge, pass another post with yellow arrows and a cottage over on your right, then reach a crossing bridleway.

2 Turn left, ignoring a bridleway on the immediate left. Later you pass another bridleway on the right and continue on the main, shingle-surfaced track as it twists and turns through the woods. The shingle runs out and the track becomes grassy as you start to climb into a more open area, keeping to the left of a series of posts. Go over a crossing bridleway and continue to the top of the slope where you'll find a handy bench over on the right.

Rest awhile and take in the marvellous panoramic views – Redlands to the west, the North Downs beyond Dorking straight ahead, with the spire of Ranmore church on the horizon, and the Betchworth Hills and the former Brockham quarries to the east.

At the same time, try to imagine Holmwood Common, once part of the old Manor of Dorking held by King Harold, as it would have been a century or two ago. It was a wild and woody, inaccessible place, a haunt of smugglers and sheep-stealers. The toll road linking Dorking with Horsham, built in 1755, made crossing the Common easier but highwaymen were still active for another 50 years or so. The Common, acquired by the National Trust in 1956, was the gift of the Duke of Norfolk whose forebears had owned it since the early 17th century.

3 Facing your original direction up the slope, midway between two posts go straight ahead on a small, unsigned footpath which soon curves to the left and then bears left onto a wide track coming in from the right. Shortly reach a post where you turn right through a barrier and then, almost immediately, bear left onto a footpath. Your path soon curves to the right and goes over a crossing track. (There's a large house over on your left.) You go down a slope and, immediately after crossing a bridge, reach a T-junction.

4 Turn left, soon going over a driveway, and pass in front of some tile-hung houses, including Clematis Cottage and The Old Cottage. At the ensuing T-junction turn left and shortly fork left over a sleeper bridge, immediately turning right then left up a grassy bridleway. Soon go over a crossing bridleway and almost immediately turn right onto a parallel, wide grassy footpath. Continue over some sleepers, through two barriers, past a post, under power lines and bear right over a broad track at a multi-

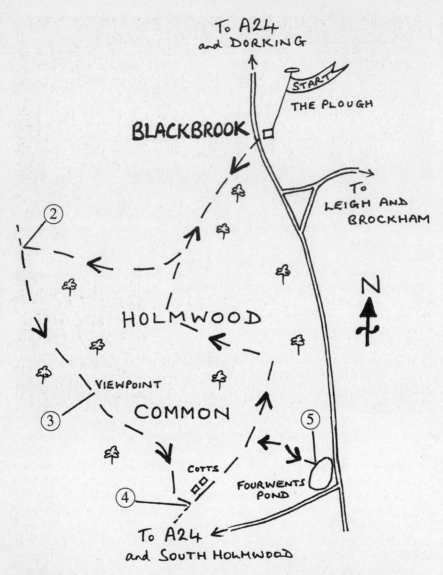

TO A24
and DORKING

START
THE PLOUGH

BLACKBROOK

TO
LEIGH AND
BROCKHAM

②

HOLMWOOD

N

VIEWPOINT

③

COMMON

⑤

COTTS

④

FOURWENTS
POND

TO A24
and SOUTH HOLMWOOD

arrowed post. Maintain direction onto a more narrow footpath, shortly going over a footbridge and boardwalk. A couple of planks (if they are still there!) take you over a ditch and you arrive at Fourwents Pond. Usually there are fishermen dotted around and an abundance of waterfowl, including swans and mallards with onshore geese. If it's quiet when you arrive you might even see a heron.

Fourwents Pond, Holmwood Common.

5   From the pond retrace your steps over the grassy area and plank bridge to the boardwalk and footbridge. You arrive back at the multi-arrowed post and take the footpath (yellow arrow) going diagonally left. Shortly you reach a crossing bridleway and turn right, following the track under power cables. Pass another bridleway turning on the left and shortly your track curves to the left away from the cables. Cross a ditch and in another ¼ mile pass a post and a path forking to the left. Shortly you reach another post, where you go over a crossing track and soon over another. Ignore a fork to the right and at the next post you arrive at a T-junction. Turn left down a slope and, in 100 yards or so, at the next post, turn sharply right onto another bridleway, which continues downhill. As your track curves right, leave the bridleway at the next post and drop down to a lower footpath, on which you turn right, back onto your outward route. In a ¼ mile you'll find yourself back at the pub.

15 Brockham
The Royal Oak

The Royal Oak (Ind Coope), facing onto Brockham's green which has the largest Guy Fawkes' Night bonfire in Surrey, is frequented by local people as well as visitors. There's been a pub on the site since the mid 18th century, the cellar being the original one, but the main building only dates from Victorian times. Walkers are particularly welcome and if they use the Villagers' Bar on the left, with its linoleum-covered floor, they don't even need to remove their boots – dogs are permitted there, too. The Saloon Bar on the right has diners in mind and you will need more than a minute or two to consider all the menu choices.

There is something for everyone. For those on a budget there are five ploughman's choices and the triple-decker 'Royal Oak Club Sandwiches' offer a filling alternative. If you are seeking a substantial meal you need look no further than the 'tasty pie slices', or there are hot oven bakes, jacket potatoes, steaks and grills, several choices of seafood and poultry as well as salads, rice and vegetarian dishes. Children are not forgotten and have their own 'kiddies' corner'. For those with appetites not fully satiated there's also a fine choice of puddings. The real ales travel from all over the south and east of England to join one of the best selections anywhere in the county. The names on the pumps are Adnams, Wadworth 6X, Young's Special, Greene King Abbot and Harvey's Sussex. There's a choice of two draught ciders, Taunton Cidermaster or Thurston Blackthorn, and draught Guinness. All the beers and ciders are well cared for in an extremely large and beautifully cool cellar. Five white wines and one claret are available by the glass, and a selection of bottled European and New World wines are kept in prime condition. There's a pleasant outlook over the green from the seats and tables in front of the pub and children's amusements can be found in the beer garden to the rear. Accompanied children who are eating are welcome inside.

The pub is open on Monday to Friday from 11 am to 3 pm and 6 pm to 11 pm, on Saturday from 11 am to 11 pm, and on Sunday from 12 noon to 10.30 pm. Food (full menu) is served on Monday to Friday from 12 noon to 2 pm and 7 pm to 9 pm (9.30 pm on Friday), on Saturday from 12 noon to 2.30 pm and 7 pm to 9.30 pm, and on Sunday from 12 noon to 2.30 pm. A restricted menu is available on Saturday from 3 pm to 5 pm and on Sunday from 3 pm to 5 pm and 7 pm to 9 pm.

Telephone: 01737 843241.

How to get there: Brockham is just off the A25, south-east of Dorking. From the M25 leave at junction 8 (travelling clockwise) or junction 9 (anti-clockwise) and make your way to the parallel A25. Brockham is signposted 1 mile from Dorking or 3 miles from Reigate. Once you have crossed the bridge over the river, turn left along the green and find the pub almost immediately on the left.

Parking: There is a car park behind the pub which you are welcome to use whilst on your walk, but please let them know. You are advised not to park in the little roads in front of the pub as this causes congestion.

Length of the walk: About 3 miles, which can be reduced by about ½ mile. OS maps: Landranger 187 Dorking and Reigate or Pathfinders 1226 Dorking, 1206 Woking and Leatherhead, 1207 Caterham and Epsom Downs and (very small part only) 1227 Horley and Gatwick Airport (inn GR 197496).

This route features two separate facets of Surrey's countryside – the more gentle flat walking around Brockham itself and the wilder open spaces of the North Downs on the other side of the A25. A short climb rewards you with a wonderful panoramic view over wide stretches of the central part of the county.

The Walk

1   From the pub turn left along the green, soon passing another pub, the Duke's Head. Besides being the site of the famous annual bonfire, the green was regularly used for cricket at one time and well-known players,

including W. G. Grace, played here. You reach a large white gate and to the right of this will discover an ancient pound where animals were held until their owners had paid a 'fine' to the Lord of the Manor to allow them to graze on the green. To the left is a smaller gate leading you onto a tarred path and over a small footbridge, then a more substantial one across the river Mole. The river acquired the name due to its habit of partially going underground in times of drought. Brockham is a name associated with badgers, which used to abound near here, but it could well mean 'settlement by a brook'.

Bear right on the wide track ahead and, at a fork, keep left on the main track. You emerge onto a road, Mill Hill Lane, and soon cross another, Kiln Lane, passing a wooden seat on your left. Go through two metal posts and shortly join a driveway coming in from the right. Cross another road and continue on a footpath passing between a Harvester inn and a Happy Eater restaurant, going over the latter's car park to the A25.

2 Cross the road with care and go over a stile by power cables. Go straight across a field, under the cables, to another stile and a track on which you turn right, continuing along the side of a railway embankment. You reach a crossing track and turn left under the railway to arrive at two farm gates. Cross a stile on the right and go diagonally right across a field, passing pig pens. As you get close to an electricity pylon turn left on an upward-sloping track running between fields and aim for a stile by a metal gate in the trees ahead. You have a choice here.

For the shorter walk, turn left along the track and in about ¼ mile reach the limeworks at Point 4. Although this will avoid a steep downward slope you will miss a magnificent view.

To complete the full walk, continue as follows:

3 After crossing the stile turn right on a woodland path and, a few yards after the fence on the right runs out, you reach a fork and bear left. Ignore a small opening on the left and continue past a disused pit and large mound on your left. You reach a T-junction by a green-banded post, number 4, and turn left onto a section of the North Downs Way, initially taking the lower and then joining the higher path. In about 200 yards you reach a sloping crossing track where you turn left. This path is fairly steep and can be slippery after rain so take advantage of the useful conifer branches by holding on to them as you carefully descend. Before arriving at the bottom of the slope you will find a right turn leading onto a more level path and will shortly reach a magnificent, yet very isolated, viewpoint.

After taking in the views you continue to a fork. Mercifully, you take the left one, not the little path going steeply down and up again. At a junction of several small paths continue forward and begin to descend once more, keeping to the main track. You reach a wooden fence and a right turning but keep forward to arrive at a wooden gate where you cross

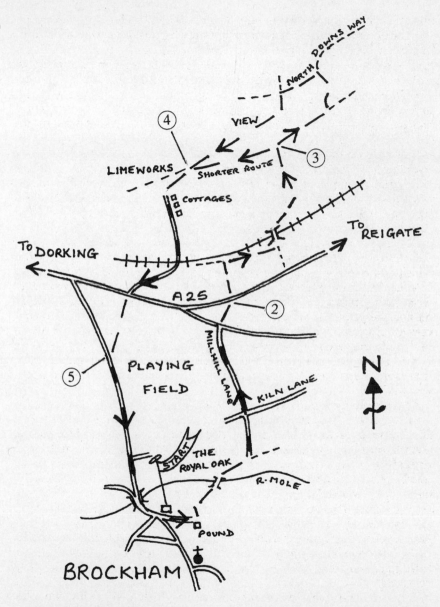

a stile. At the immediate T-junction, turn left over another stile. You reach yet another stile by a gate and turn left, shortly entering the former Brockham Limeworks.

These limeworks are part of Surrey's industrial heritage and for a

Footbridge at Brockham.

century or more were a hive of frantic activity. The County Council is attempting to preserve the site and some rebuilding has taken place. Spare a few minutes from the walk to explore the place and you will discover an extremely deep pit, covered by an iron grille, and sheds previously holding the engines that pulled train loads of lime along a small-gauge railway system. Also on the site you'll find a board with information on the wildlife attracted to this area.

4   To continue the walk, go through a gate to the left of one of the sheds, leading you onto a roadway. You pass some cottages on the left and have good views on the right towards Leith Hill and its surrounding area. A level crossing takes you back over the railway and you bear right. Pass a field full of what look like Nissen huts for pigs, and cross the A25 again to join a footpath opposite. Eventually you come out to a road.

5   Turn left along the pavement, passing Brockham Big Field recreation ground. Go over Kiln Lane again and cross to the other side of the road. An attractive new footbridge, running parallel with the renovated road bridge, takes you back over the river Mole. You reach Brockham Green and bear left to return to the pub.

16 Reigate Heath
The Skimmington Castle

The Skimmington Castle (Pubmaster) was built of wattle and daub – a mixture of lime and cow manure – around 1600. Originally called Downes Farm, it later became Skeffington, the name of the settlement which later became Skimmington. The 1877 edition of *Kelly's Directory* lists the owner as one James Bonny who, besides retailing beer, manufactured mineral water in a nearby factory. The building incorporated a chimney for curing hams and a bread oven, and these are still much in evidence today. Later the pub was sold to a brewery and over the past century has passed from one brewing company to another.

The pub today has four separate rooms, each with its own character. Nothing is uniform and the assortment of chairs and tables helps create a pleasant, relaxed ambience. No fruit machines here. From the most recent addition to the pub, the front bar, you can enjoy the best views towards the North Downs, particularly when the trees are leafless in winter. The rear bar, however, is probably the most cosy of them all, with its inglenook fireplace. It is said that a century or two ago highwaymen climbed the chimney and used it as a lookout for coaches travelling the turnpike between Reigate and Dorking, the present A25. From this room there are doors marked 'Tool Shed' and 'Potting Shed', the latter leading down some steps to the family room.

The cuisine is certainly a cut above the average pub grub, all the pie pastry being home-made with local grocers, fishmongers and butchers supplying the produce to go in it. The finished products are extremely tasty, filling and beautifully presented. If you are sampling one of the daily changing specials, which may include uncommon choices such as minted lamb pie, lamb shanks or gammon knuckles, be warned – don't order a pud before finishing the main course. Chances are you won't have room for it! Even something lighter, for example one of the ten different sandwiches (hand-cut from granary or farmhouse loaves), or a choice of five ploughman's lunches, will provide a most satisfying meal. This is a pub for the real-ale drinking connoisseur. Besides Burton and Boddingtons and Flowers, you'll find a Whitbread lighter ale, Fuggles. Unusual guest ales may include Dr Pepper's Lemon Ale and many other exotic brews. Draught cider drinkers have a choice of three – Cidermaster, Dry Blackthorn and Addlestone's, and Guinness comes through a pump, too. The extensive wine list describes 28 to 30 different labels. For those preferring to drink their pints outside there are some tables and chairs at the front. Visitors with children who wish to dine inside are encouraged to use the family room. Dogs on leads are permitted in the pub.

The pub is open on Monday to Friday from 11 am to 2.30 pm and 6 pm to 11 pm, on Saturday from 11 am to 3 pm and 6 pm to 11 pm, and on Sunday from 12 noon to 3 pm and 7 pm to 10.30 pm. Food is served on Monday to Saturday from 12 noon to 2.30 pm and 7 pm to 9.30 pm, and on Sunday from 12 noon to 2.30 pm (no food on Sunday evening at the time of our visit).

Telephone: 01737 243100.

How to get there: Leave the A25 west of Reigate at the Black Horse and continue on Flanchford Road. After the last house on the left you pass car parks on both sides of the road and soon reach Bonny's Road, on which you turn left. You will find the pub facing you at the end of this unmade road.

Parking: There is a large car park at the rear which, with permission, you are welcome to use whilst on your walk.

Length of the walk: About 3 miles. OS maps: Landranger 187 Dorking and Reigate or Pathfinder 1227 Horley and Gatwick Airport and, for a very small part only, 1207 Caterham and Epsom Downs (inn GR 238497).

A fine pub, some pleasant footpaths and bridleways, several excellent views, a pretty millpond and an impressive windmill, now converted into an unusual church, combine to make this a pleasant walking experience at any time of the year.

The Walk

1   From the pub turn right down a slope to a set of fingerposts. The left one points to 'Link 4' – this is one of five paths that join the Greensand Way with the North Downs Way. However, you turn right onto the Greensand Way, which later slopes up and then down to a metal fingerpost indicating three directions. Turn right on the concreted farm track forming the footpath signed to Rice Bridge. After passing a large barn bear right, then left, past Littleton Manor Farm and along the side of a field. Cross a stile and bear diagonally left across another field to the stile in the corner. Continue on an enclosed path offering good views to the south and reach a road with Littleton Nursing Home on your right.

2   Cross the road to a bridleway opposite, signposted to Rice Bridge and Wonham Lane. Later bear right past the attractively tile-hung Gilbert's Farm house, shortly ignoring the footpath on the left leading to Rice Bridge. Continue ahead and, after passing along the edge of a wood, the track bears left and you reach a four-way fingerpost. Turn right in the direction of the public footpath finger and go over a stile into a field. You soon cross two more stiles each side of a snatch of woods and continue along the edge of another field. After passing a house on your left you join a driveway and cross a grass triangle to reach a road.

3   Turn left, switching sides as necessary and, where the road curves left, ignore a footpath turning on the right. Shortly you will pass Wonham Cottage on the right and, almost immediately, go up some steps onto a public footpath leading past the most attractive Wonham Mill house and pond.

4   Immediately after going over the millrace and under a willow tree, do not proceed to the road ahead but cross a stile on the right taking you into a large field. Having gone straight across the field, you will reach a stile, then soon cross another by a large barn and come to a farm track.

5   Turn right on the track which runs through Dungate's Farm and forms part of the Greensand Way, the long-distance route on which you commenced your walk.

The Greensand Way, which is your path for the remainder of the walk, is one of Surrey's two main walking routes, the other being the North Downs Way. The Surrey section of the Greensand Way runs 55 miles from Haslemere, close to the border with West Sussex, ending just beyond Limpsfield Chart on the Kent border. It embraces the county's and, indeed, the south-east's highest point at Leith Hill (almost 1,000 ft). The route was devised by the late Geoffrey Hollis who, for many years, presented walks in the *Surrey Advertiser*.

After passing through the farmyard, keep ahead on the track, later with the babbling Pipp Brook accompanying you on the left. At a Y-junction bear right through a gate and cross a field, soon going through another gate and keeping ahead on a track. You reach a cottage and cross a fairway

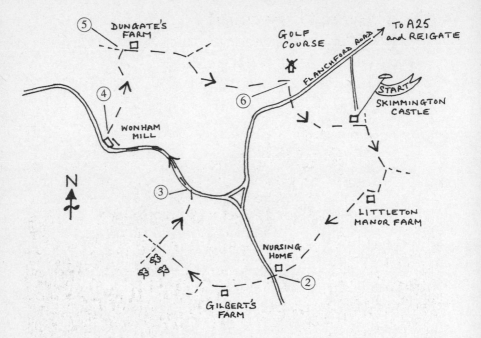

on Reigate Heath golf course and then go up the sandy footpath ahead to the right of the clubhouse and a windmill.

Reigate Heath Mill, which dates from 1765, ceased working in 1868 and was converted into a chapel 20 years later. In 1962 the dilapidated mill was restored by the local council. Now known as the Mill Church, services are held here on the third Sunday of each month at 3 pm.

6 Follow the track to the right of the buildings and 10 to 12 yards before it bears left, turn right and ignore an immediate right fork. Continue downhill on a sandy footpath, going over a couple of crossing paths and down to a road.

Cross the road to go along the lane opposite. At the end of the lane continue ahead up a footpath and along the edge of a wood. Keep ahead, passing Ivy Cottage, and then go along the footpath alongside Tilehouse Cottage. Follow the path past Heathfield Nursery, with its considerable choice of flower pots, and soon you are back at the pub.

17 Lower Kingswood
The Mint Arms

The Mint Arms (freehouse) takes its name from the fields of herbs, including mint, which were once a feature of the area. The present building went up soon after the First World War on the site of a former pub and has now been considerably extended. The bars are comfortable and roomy and walkers are made to feel most welcome. There is a spacious dining room and a permanent barbecue has been set up in the large, enclosed garden, which also includes a children's playing area containing a wealth of equipment.

Besides a restaurant menu, there is a blackboard displaying many 'Chef's Specials', which include a roast of the day and lighter items such as grilled sardines with a salad garnish. Fresh cut sandwiches are made to order and hot baguettes, ploughman's lunches and salads are always obtainable. As long as good specimens can be found, jacket potatoes with a wide range of fillings are on offer. There is also a children's menu. All the vegetables are bought fresh locally and a major proportion of the food is home-cooked, including the pies for dessert. Weather permitting, the barbecue operates all summer, on Saturday and Sunday from noon until 8.30 pm and on Monday to Friday between 6 pm and 8.30 pm.

An interesting range of regular real ale is on offer, including London Pride, King & Barnes' Sussex, and Courage and Gale's best bitters, as well as the Hogs Back Brewery's TEA and usually two or three others. There's also a comprehensive wine list. When not outside, accompanied children are welcome in the restaurant. Dogs on leads are permitted in the bars and garden, but not in the restaurant.

The pub is open on Monday to Saturday from 11 am to 11 pm. On Sunday the hours are from 12 noon to 10.30 pm but drinks are only available with food between 3 pm and 7 pm. Food is served on Monday to Friday from 12 noon to 2.30 pm and 7 pm to 10 pm, on Saturday from 12 noon to 3 pm and 7 pm to 10.30 pm, and on Sunday from 12 noon to 9 pm.

Telephone: 01737 242957.

How to get there: Lower Kingswood lies just west of the A217 between Sutton and Reigate. From junction 8 of the M25, go north on the A217 (Brighton Road). In ½ mile, at a roundabout, turn left on Stubbs Lane. In ¼ mile you reach a crossroads and turn left to find the the pub immediately on the left.

Parking: There is a large car park which, with permission, you are welcome to use whilst on the walk.

Length of the walk: About 2½ miles. OS maps: Landranger 187 Dorking and Reigate or Pathfinder 1207 Caterham and Epsom Downs (inn GR 248532).

A few minutes only and suburbia is left behind as you go over fields to a stretch of ancient woodland. After crossing the M25 motorway you suddenly find yourself on a wonderful hilltop site offering almost unbelievable views over just about half the county. Linger a while and see how many well-known Surrey landmarks you can recognise. At the very least, you'll have no difficulty in spotting the south-east's highest point at Leith Hill.

The Walk
1   From the pub turn right, back to the crossroads, and then turn left along the pavement for about ¼ mile. At the last house, Appledore, turn left over a stile by a public footpath signpost and continue along the side of a field. Cross another stile and a farm track. Go over the stile ahead to pass Dent's Farm and walk along the side of the next field, reaching a stile in a hedge at a four-way fingerpost.
2   After crossing the stile bear right to maintain direction along a roadway which passes the car park serving visitors to the National Trust's Margery Wood.

This woodland is all that remains of what was a considerably larger, ancient forest and contains mainly mature oak and beech which have been in-filled with birch. If you can take time out of the walk proper in the appropriate season (April/May) to enjoy the bluebells, you're in for a treat. Much of the original land, which came from various donors, was lost to that great monument to the 20th century, the London Orbital Motorway – the infamous M25.

Continue the walk by crossing the motorway, now eight lanes, shortly arriving at a gate and an opening onto Reigate Hill. Go forward over the green, immediately crossing the North Downs Way.

Over to your left you will notice a circular building, a little like a miniature Georgian pavilion. If you go across to see it in more detail, you'll find it's a small, roofed seating area with a blue ceiling picked out with gold stars. It was presented to the Corporation of the Borough of Reigate for the benefit of the public by Lieutenant-Colonel Robert William Inglis in 1909.

3 To continue the walk, turn right along the side of Colley Hill, also in the care of the National Trust. There are splendid views over Reigate, across the Weald, towards the South Downs. To the south-west the skyline is dominated by Leith Hill and Redlands and the view to the immediate west continues along the North Downs to the Betchworth and Brockham Hills. As you walk along the pleasant, undulating path, close to

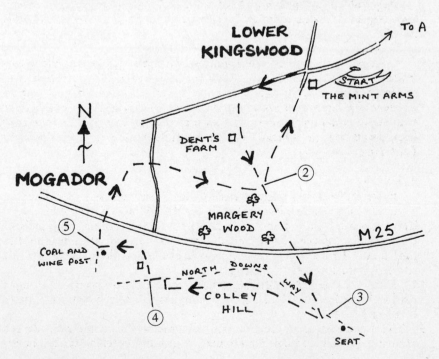

the edge of the escarpment, try to spot other landmarks. At one point, through the trees you should be able to make out a windmill on Reigate Heath which you pass close by on Walk 16.

Go through a gap in a hedge and pass a water tower with various antennae, over on your right. After a total of ½ mile or so, reach a point where the hill dips down quite dramatically. It's time to leave all the wonderful views behind you and join the path turning right into the trees (not the one going diagonally right as this becomes extremely overgrown with brambles in high summer). You soon reach the North Downs Way once more and turn left along it for a short distance.

4   Immediately after passing a NT sign for Colley Hill and the start of a path on the left, the potentially brambly one you avoided a few minutes ago, turn right through some concrete posts and onto a roadway. Continue past a large house, The Old Pheasantry and, at a T-junction, go left along another roadway, Merrywood Grove. The roar of traffic on the M25, nearby on your right, will be apparent again by now. You reach a road and, if you look carefully over to the left, may spot a white metal post.

This is a rather sad-looking example, but there are a prolific number of these little pieces of history in the area. Coal and Wine Posts, as they were named, were erected in 1851 to mark the boundaries of the Metropolitan Police District where tolls were levied on coal and wine being taken into London. They were usually about 20 miles from the City and were in use until 1889.

5   Turn right along the road, back over the M25, and in about ¼ mile, immediately after passing a house called Thornymoor, turn right on a bridleway signposted '½ mile to Margery Lane'. You cross a lane to the bridleway opposite and the farmhouse you passed much earlier in the walk, Dent's Farm, comes into view on the left. At the end of the bridleway don't go over the stile you crossed earlier but this time turn left up the rough lane, which later becomes tarred and brings you back to the pub.

18 Chipstead
The Ramblers Rest

The Ramblers Rest (Whitbread) was once a farmhouse and there are records of its owners since the beginning of the 14th century. It has been used as a hostelry of sorts since Elizabethan times and retained the name Dene Farm when it became a traditional country inn and more recently a restaurant. Since 1993 it has been a family pub with a more welcoming name. The main building is Grade II listed and the adjacent barn Grade I.

The premises have been tastefully refurbished and retain a medieval feel, with ancient exposed brick and flint walls and ceiling beams. There are two large bar areas with panelled walls and a separate restaurant but it's pleasant to be able to eat wherever you choose to sit. The rambling connection is reflected in the display of walking gear more commonly used at least half a century ago, with a traditional haversack, gaiters, boots and a walking stick. The small exhibition of artefacts from yesteryear is completed with old lemonade bottles and Brownie cameras. There is a lovely garden at the rear of the inn, with an ancient dovecote complete with doves.

The pub's regular menu is extensive and you can get something to eat from the 'lighter bites' section at almost any time the bars are open. You will find such things as traditional cheese ploughman's lunches, doorstep sandwiches (thinner ones available on request) and steak and kidney pudding as well! A large percentage of the food is home-prepared and at lunchtime and in the evening there's a good range of grills and other popular dishes, a selection of vegetarian meals, a children's menu and a choice of desserts. The menu prices are the same wherever you eat but in the restaurant you'll receive waitress service and also be tempted by a gourmet specials board. Real ale aficionados are spoilt for choice. Besides the regular threesome of Boddingtons, Flowers and London Pride, there are five others changing regularly, four of which have their barrels behind the bar. Both Guinness and Murphy's stouts come through taps as well as Bulmer's Original cider and a Muscadet medium dry white wine. Well-behaved children are welcome in the pub, as are dogs on leads.

The pub is open on Monday to Saturday from 11 am to 11 pm, and on Sunday from 12 noon to 10.30 pm. Food on the main and 'specials' menus is served every day from 12 noon to 3 pm and 6 pm to 9.30 pm, while 'lighter bites' are available right through from 11 am to 10 pm (9.30 pm on Sunday).

Telephone: 01737 552661.

How to get there: The pub is located on the B2032, which runs from Coulsdon and joins the A217 at the Tadworth roundabout. From Chipstead travel in a north-westerly direction on Hazelwood Lane and, after crossing a railway bridge, turn left at a T-junction onto the B2032. The pub is about ½ mile along the road on the right. Chipstead railway station is a short distance from Point 3.

Parking: The pub has car parks, front and back, which you are welcome to use whilst on your walk, but please let them know at reception.

Length of the walk: About 2 miles. OS maps: Landranger 187 Dorking and Reigate or Pathfinder 1207 Caterham and Epsom Downs (inn GR 273575).

This short walk introduces you to another of Surrey's well-loved open spaces and ancient woodlands, providing some excellent views over the Chipstead Valley and to the Downs beyond. If you plan to eat at the pub and need to work up more of an appetite, extend the walk by following one of the nature trails described on the notice board when you reach the car park at Point 3.

The Walk

1 From the pub go past the ancient wooden barn, turning left through the main car park behind, and continue through the fence ahead to join a path signposted for the Banstead Countryside Walk (one of the nature trails mentioned above). Follow this wide grassy path which gently

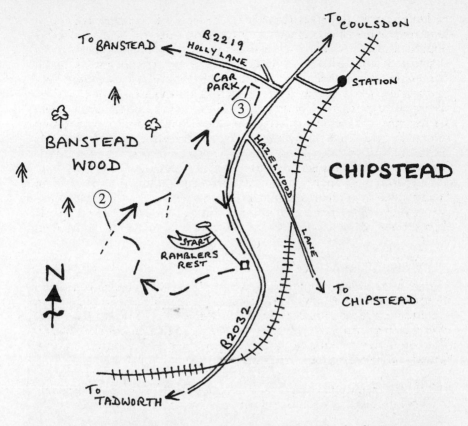

ascends. After about ¼ mile the path curves to the right, leading you over a crossing track and across a field towards a line of trees. After going through an archway formed by oaks, turn right along the side of a large field, curving left as you reach the corner and staying at the field edge until you arrive at a wooden post near a fence and gate.

2 Turn right, back onto the Banstead Countryside Walk, shortly reaching another post and entering Banstead Wood between venerable beech trees. You'll also find oak, sweet chestnut, hawthorn and many other species as you commence your descent. At a fork take either path and, in a few yards, join another path on which you bear left and come to a three-way fingerpost. Follow the sign to Holly Lane.

You'll soon find a handy bench on which to sit for a while to take in the view over the Chipstead Valley. A dead tree sculpture dominates the scene. One of Chipstead's most famous sons was Sir Edward Banks who built the original London Bridge, now sadly moved to the United States. Another of his bridges crossing the Thames to Waterloo was also replaced but his Southwark Bridge remains.

Continue on, shortly reaching another post at a gate, and keep ahead on the downward slope where the views open out. At the next three-way fingerpost bear right in the direction of the Holly Lane car park. In the car park you will find public toilets and a notice board describing the area and some of the paths within it.

3 Facing the road ahead, turn right out of the car park, going through a gate midway along a fence and in about 50 yards reach a path going off to the right, with an elm cabin over on your left. Turn right along this path, soon entering woodland and, as you emerge, join a tarred path running parallel with the road on the left. By a large sycamore tree you'll find a white metal post. There are many of these posts in this part of Surrey and in the 19th century they indicated the boundary of the area where tolls were due from those bringing coal and wine into London.

Continue ahead, going through a large gate or over a stile, and soon find yourself back at the pub.

Journey's end – the lovely garden at the Ramblers Rest.

19 Old Coulsdon
The Fox

The Fox (Bass) claims to have been yet another stopping off place for England's most infamous highwayman, Dick Turpin. He certainly got around, his highway robberies seeming to have been punctuated by the 18th-century equivalent of a pub crawl.

The inn today owes much of its popularity to the fact that it stands right on the edge of some lovely walking country. One large room forms a spacious lounge bar with plenty of seating and a corner given over to a public bar. To remind you of the name, a taxidermist's skill is well in evidence in the shape of a fox. Also encased in glass are reminders that Crystal Palace is the home team.

A wide range of food is always available. The 'Hungryman's Burger' – a double-decker with burger, bacon and cheese, complete with chips – is always popular. So is the traditional sizzling 8 oz steak served with peas, tomatoes, mushrooms, onion rings and fries. There are other grills and hot meals as well as the usual favourites like ploughman's lunches, salads and sandwiches. Vegetarians are not forgotten and children have their own menu. Regularly changing specials, such as roast chicken and fisherman's pie, are shown on the blackboard and there are desserts, too. With a little notice, special dietary needs can be accommodated. The regular real ale is Fuller's London Pride and another two or three, such as Greene King IPA, are changed frequently. Draught Red Rock cider, draught Guinness and medium and dry white wines are all on tap. Well-behaved children are welcome in the dining area but dogs are not allowed in the pub. Outside there's a small paved area with seating under a tree where dogs are permitted. At lunchtime on Sunday during the summer children are entertained in the enclosed garden with a magician and a bouncy castle.

The pub is open on Monday to Saturday from 11 am to 11 pm, and on Sunday from 12 noon to 10.30 pm. Food is served on Monday to Saturday from 11.30 am to 10 pm, and on Sunday from 12 noon to 10 pm.

Telephone: 01883 344643.

How to get there: The pub is situated on the southern side of Coulsdon Common, just off the B2030 which runs between the A23 at Coulsdon and the A22 at Caterham. It is about 2 miles equidistant from each place.

Parking: There is a large car park which you are welcome to use whilst on the walk. If this is full, just beyond there is a parking area by the green and another large car park a few yards further on from that.

Length of the walk: About 3 miles. OS maps: Landranger 187 Dorking and Reigate or Pathfinder 1207 Caterham and Epsom Downs (inn GR 318568).

This undulating walk leads you from Coulsdon Common down to Happy Valley, which runs to Farthing Downs and over fields to a very ancient church with a famous wall painting. An information board with a map, which you pass at the start of the walk, provides further ideas for exploring the area, time permitting.

The Walk

1 From the pub rejoin the roadway and turn left, continuing ahead past a fingerpost pointing to Farthing Downs, so called because of the Roman coins or 'farthings' found there in considerable numbers. Pass a car park and a notice board giving information on this area, go through a gateway and continue on a track running along the side of a large field. In about ⅓ mile, at the end of the field, descend through some trees and, after some 100 yards, reach a three-way fingerpost.

2 Turn left on the path to Ditches Lane and descend into Happy Valley, partially aided by some steps on the left. In the valley bottom go over parallel crossing tracks and up the other side on the path signposted to Chaldon church. Pass a bench on the right and go through a snatch of woodland, then continue diagonally left across a large arable field. Pass close to a peninsular belt of trees on the edge of Figgs Wood and maintain direction over the field. At the far side go under some more trees and out

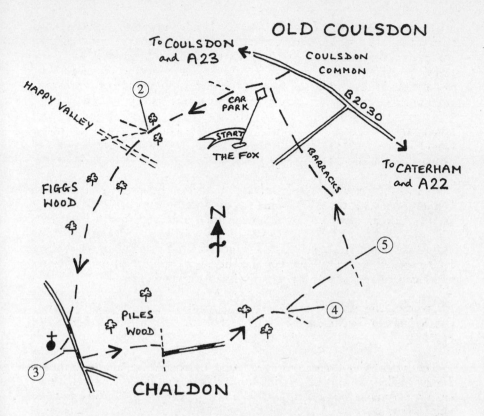

to Ditches Lane. Turn left and, in a few yards, right to Chaldon church.

The church, dedicated to St Peter and St Paul, is of Saxon foundation and contains many treasures. Inside, on the west wall, is a remarkable 12th-century wall painting which depicts the 'Ladder of Salvation of the Human Soul'. The souls of men are drawn as naked figures attempting to climb from Hell in the lower part towards purgatory and Christ in Heaven at the top. The painting measures 17ft 2in by 11ft 2in and was not discovered, under whitewash, until workmen were renovating the church in 1870. Also to be seen is a stone coffin lid from the 12th century, and a tablet inscribed in 1562.

3 From the church fork right, back to the lane. Turn right for a few yards, where you turn left on a footpath signposted to Piles Wood. Continue along the edge of the field you crossed earlier, later with the wood on your left and, in ¼ mile, reach a T-junction. Turn right and immediately left along a residential road, Leazes Avenue. The gardens on the left each have a magnificent redwood, suggesting that at one time this road may have been an impressive avenue. At the end of the road continue

The church of St Peter and St Paul, Chaldon.

on a bridleway, ignoring an immediate right fork. Go down into a valley and up again, through trees. At the top of the slope pass along the edge of a field and arrive at a three-way fingerpost by the remains of a stile.

4 Bear left, continuing on the bridleway, over the remains of a wall and down into another valley. You then ascend a staircase of tree roots and continue on a track running between fields, arriving at a T-junction in front of a new housing estate.

5 Turn left along a track, shortly going along the side of the former Caterham Barracks, built in 1877, once the famous depot of the Coldstream Guards. After passing the barracks complex, cross over a road, continue straight ahead, ignoring a path forking left, and soon arrive back at the pub.

20 Bletchingley
The Prince Albert

The Prince Albert (freehouse), dating from the 15th century, stands in the wide village High Street with its picturesque tile-hung buildings. The interior, with its exposed beams, is cosy and welcoming, and the pub is popular with locals and visitors alike. On entering you will find a small, traditional country pub bar. To one side is a non-smoking dining room and, on the other, a larger bar/eating area, which leads to an intimate dining room where smoking is permitted. The landlord's passion for vintage cars is evident in the prints, as well as the polished engine parts, that adorn the walls.

If you like something a little different from normal pub grub you will be in for a real treat here. The chef's creativity extends to dishes with a colonial Portuguese, Far Eastern or Continental influence but he aims to please all tastes, be they for basic steak, chips and peas or more adventurous fare. The regular mid-day menu includes the usual favourites such as open sandwiches, ploughman's lunches, salads and home-made soups, or you might go for steak and kidney pudding or fillet of lemon sole filled with seafood. Evening specials include mouth-watering delights such as grilled swordfish on a base of julienne vegetables in ginger sauce or a rack of lamb. There are usually four real ales and the landlord tends to keep his options open. On our visit Marston's Pedigree and Young's

Special, as well as Surrey and Crusader from nearby Reigate's Pilgrim Brewery, were choices offered. Children are allowed into the dining areas of the pub and dogs, preferably on leads, in the bar area only. There is a pleasant, well-kept garden at the rear which patrons with children and dogs are encouraged to use on fine summer days.

The pub is open on Monday to Saturday from 11 am to 3 pm and 6 pm to 11 pm, and on Sunday from 12 noon to 3 pm and 7 pm to 10.30 pm. Food is served on Monday to Saturday from 12 noon to 2.30 pm and 6.30 pm to 9.30 pm, and on Sunday from 12 noon to 2.30 pm. No food is available on Sunday evening.

Telephone: 01883 743257.

How to get there: Bletchingley is on the A25 between Redhill and Godstone. Travelling from Redhill, you will find the pub on the right on a corner at the far end of the village. If coming from the M25, leave at junction 6 and continue on the A25 via Godstone, looking for the pub on your left immediately after entering the village.

Parking: The pub has no car park of its own but there is usually plenty of parking on each side of the wide High Street. There are no restrictions and the cobbled forecourts of the neighbouring shops and offices are for all to use.

Length of the walk: About 2½ miles. OS maps: Landranger 187 Dorking and Reigate or Pathfinder 1207 Caterham and Epsom Downs (inn GR 328507).

Soon after leaving Bletchingley's busy main street you will find wide open views over to Surrey's imposing range of hills, the North Downs. Gently sloping fields lead you down to a lane or two where you may feel traffic is almost non-existent. En route you'll be close to two attractive historic buildings and at the end of the walk you pass an impressive church of some note.

The Walk

1   From the pub cross the main road and go down Church Lane. You pass the church and will have the opportunity of seeing it much closer at the end of the walk. Go past a small housing estate built on the site of a former hospital. You'll soon see the entrance to Bletchingley Golf Club and its clubhouse on your right. Turn left on a footpath running along the side of the golf course with a fence on your right. There are now good views across to the North Downs as you reach a three-way fingerpost.

2   Turn right over a stile onto a grassy path running alongside the golfing fairways, with a line of trees on your left. At the end of the golf course go

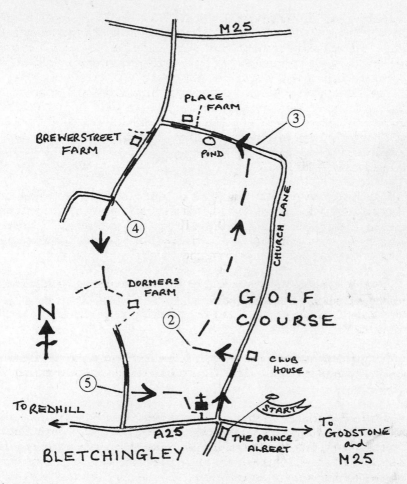

through the trees and down to cross a stile. Now you come to a fair hurdle course of stiles taking you across a very large field. Although the traffic on the M25 is well in sight and coming ever closer there is, mercifully, little evidence of its drone. After crossing the last stile you reach a lane and a fingerpost.

3   Turn left along the lane and shortly, if you look through the fence on your left, you'll discover an attractive pond. Very soon you pass a footpath turning on your right and arrive at the entrance to Place Farm. This was once the gatehouse and is now the only remnant of Bletchingley Place, a grand manor house given to Anne of Cleves on her divorce from Henry VIII. Continue to the end of the lane and a T-junction where you turn left. In a few moments, on your right, you'll see the most impressive

Brewer Street Farm, Bletchingley.

Brewer Street Farm. Dating from 1430, it was originally a yeoman farmer's house. The roof is covered in Horsham slates. Continue down the lane to where it turns sharply right by Perkins Cottage.

4 Leave the lane by continuing straight ahead onto a footpath, shortly going through a metal barrier. You pass footpath turnings to the right, then left, then go through another metal barrier and past the entrance to Dormers Farm. Here you join a footpath running above and alongside a road. You pass some houses and discover a footpath alongside a small engineering works.

5 Turn left here and continue on the enclosed footpath, going through a barrier. Eventually you come to the edge of the small housing estate you passed at the beginning of the walk and reach the churchyard via a gate. Fork right, passing Bletchingley church on your left. This fine parish church is used by the three denominations, Anglican, Catholic and Methodist, and dates from Norman times, but was largely rebuilt in the 1600s. Leave the churchyard by the gate ahead and arrive at a short road leading back to the High Street and the pub.

Bletchingley and its former market place were once dominated by a large castle, to the south, which was destroyed in a battle in 1264. Before the 1832 franchise reforms, the 100 or so electors returned two MPs – making it a 'rotten borough'.

MATT DICKINSON

Killer Storm.

A special thank you to Sarah Darby
for the chapter heading illustrations.

Also by Matt Dickinson

Mortal Chaos

Black Ice

The Death Zone

The Everest Files

North Face

Lie Kill Walk Away